PENMAENMAWR

Rails of Granite

by

Mike Hitches

IRWELL
PRESS

PENMAENMAWR AND WELSH GRANITE CO.

LIMITED.

The Quarries are situated at

PENMAENMAWR and TREVOR, nr. Carnarvon.

The **STONE** supplied for the maintenance and construction of Roads has been known and used for over **SEVENTY YEARS** with the **BEST RESULTS.**

The regularly increasing demand for it proves that its practical value is continually being more and more appreciated.

It is **TOUGH, HARD, ADHESIVE, IMPERVIOUS TO MOISTURE,** and sustains the wear and tear of the heaviest traffic in a **wonderfully satisfactory manner.**

The Company makes all sizes of **SETTS, SELF-FACED** and **TOOLED KERBS** and **CHANNELS** and **WHEELERS; MACADAM, CHIPPINGS, FERRO-CONCRETE MATERIAL, BREAKERS,** and **RAILWAY BALLAST.**

TARRED MACADAM MANUFACTURED BY UP-TO-DATE AND APPROVED PLANTS. A SPECIAL FEATURE.

Orders are supplied by **RAIL, SEA** and **CANAL.**

Head Office—

PENMAENMAWR, where all communications will receive promptest attention.

Telephone No. 11 and 43.   *Telegrams*—" Granite, Penmaenmawr."

LIVERPOOL—	CARDIFF—	SOUTHERN AGENTS—
No. 4 Harrington Street.	No. 18 Quay Street.	BRITISH MACADAMS LTD.,
		No. 122 Cannon Street, London, E.C.
Telegrams—" Pavement, Liverpool."	*Telegrams*—" Granite, Cardiff."	*Telegrams*—" Propotmac, Cannon, London."
Telephone—Nos. 4957-8 Bank.	*Telephone*—No. 1970 Cardiff.	*Telephone*—No. 3421 City.

Published by
IRWELL PRESS
3, Durley Avenue, Pinner, Middlesex, HA5 1JQ
Printed by the Amadeus Press Ltd
Huddersfield, West Yorkshire

CONTENTS

FOREWORD

The railway network of this country was created for economic reasons and not so that enthusiasts could, at a later date, collect the names and numbers of engines that ran upon it. There are plenty of books which concentrate upon the engineering technicalities of 'trains' but not enough which recognise the economic and political reasons for the establishment of a railway line, and perhaps still fewer which trace the secondary effects upon parts of the country relatively isolated from the main areas of expansion of the last century.

In this work Mike Hitches relates the story of how a railway created specifically to shorten the journey from London to Dublin dramatically changed the pattern of life in a small parish in North Wales. The railway speeded up the development of the quarries and was the direct influence in the creation of a 'new town', which was to become one of the most fashionable seaside resorts in Victorian Wales. Mike also notes the decline of the town's fortunes and it is sad to note that the publication of this volume coincides with the reduction of the station to an unmanned halt.

It is a fascinating story and we are fortunate to have a 'local' to undertake the task. The book is a result of careful and enthusiastic research and I trust it will inspire others to write about their own village stations and consider the effects they had upon the social and economic life of their community.

Dennis J. Roberts,
Chairman, Penmaenmawr Historical Society.

ACKNOWLEDGEMENTS

This book could not have been written without the help of people from the local community, especially Mr. Dennis Roberts of Penmaenmawr Historical Society, who provided much of the background material on the town and directed me to some of those people who could provide other useful information.

Others whose help was important were William Roberts, who gave details of the 1917 incident, Reg Lunt, who was a St.John Ambulance worker at the 1950 accident, Peter Moss, Wendy and Maelgwyn Williams, Gwyn Roberts and Ron Watson-Jones.

Railway staff who assisted me in my research included Dave Hill and Keith Roberts, the last two staff members on the station, the now retired signalman at Penmaenmawr, Dick Charnock, and Rodney Fitzgibbon, a railwayman at Colwyn Bay.

Further material was obtained from Gwynedd Archive Service in Caernarfon, Clwyd Record Office, Hawarden, The Public Record Office Kew, Llandudno and Penmaenmawr Libraries, *The North Wales Weekly News*, *The Liverpool Daily Post*, The National Railway Museum, York and the North Wales Railway Circle. To all of these people, and others I may have omitted to mention, I offer my sincere thanks.

Finally, special thanks go to Joan and Arthur Truby for patiently checking and typing the manuscript to all of those who supplied the photographs used in this work, and to my wife, Alwen, who did not complain too much as I filled the house with increasing volumes of paper

The station around 1880. The granite sidings of the Darbishire Company are to the west and are full of loaded wagons. Land between the station and promenade is still being farmed but will soon be covered as the sidings are extended in the next few years. Station Road leading to the Penmaenmawr Hotel (in the background) is in use but the road up to the town will not be cut until 1895. The mountain has not yet been intensively quarried but developments in the crushing of stone will change its face completely over the next century

(National Railway Museum)

INTRODUCTION

Travelling by train along the North Wales coast, some 5 ½ miles west of Llandudno Junction and 10 miles east of Bangor, the railway passenger will pass through the wayside station of Penmaenmawr, with its shabby building, its modern looking signalbox and its expanse of sidings on the seaward side. As he travels through this quiet station he will not appreciate its long forgotten role in the economy of the town as tourist centre and the significance of the complex of sidings. He may not even realise that the smoothness of his journey has been made possible through the ballast under the track, which has been won from the quarries on the mountains he sees above as he passes through. This book tells of the past importance of the station, along with the development of the sidings serving the quarries, which in turn enabled the transport of the stone products so important to the town. Along with these developments came crushed stone from the quarries, much of it used as railway track ballast, with production continuing to the present day.

The story of the railway station at Penmaenmawr and its effects upon the economy of the town is, in many ways, the story of wayside stations throughout Britain. Such places have had little attention over the years; the main stations and junctions of the system in Great Britain have been well publicised as have many of the pre-Beeching branches, particularly those on the old Great Western but the wayside station, for years the lifeblood of the network, has largely been ignored, even though there have been several thousand throughout the history of railways in Britain. These stations provided employment in the towns they served and Penmaenmawr was no exception. Not only were there station staff - a station master, porters etc. but signalmen, platelayers and track maintenance men. From Penmaenmawr and round about men came for work, both in the quarries which overlooked the town and in the quarry sidings, to deal with stone trains as the complex expanded and traffic increased.

The coming of the railway disrupted the traditional economic activities in the areas in which they appeared. While the towns served by the railway expanded, those which they avoided, irrespective of any former economic success, very quickly declined. Along the North Wales coast the Chester and Holyhead Railway had enormous effect upon the traditional economies of the towns, for trade previously had largely been borne out by sea. Boats would be beached and goods loaded; once the railway was built the vessels were cut off from their sources of trade and declined rapidly. In Penmaenmawr there was a lime kiln to the east of the then parish with the lime and coal brought in by boat. When the railway came into the town the kiln could not be supplied from the sea and the Chester and Holyhead Co. took over the business. Stone setts from the slopes of Graiglwyd and Penmaenmawr, and cobblestones from the beach used as ships ballast also left the town by boat after being brought down to the shore by sledge. The coming of the railway meant that this practice could not continue as a right of way was lost. A tunnel was built under the promenade to preserve this ancient right but was never used to bring stone setts to the shore. Shipping of stone products by sea from specially constructed jetties, for many years a landmark of Penmaenmawr, continued well into the twentieth century but the railway became increasingly important as the main carrier of stone from the quarries; over the years the sidings expanded to meet this growing traffic.

Like other towns throughout the country, the establishment of the station at Penmaenmawr proved important to the development of the town and its economy and changes which have taken place through the years since it opened have been reflected on the station itself. What makes this station of such note, however, is the expanse of sidings serving the quarries, which are still there today. This, more than anything else, demonstrates the prominence of the town within the network of Britain's railways over the years and its continued importance today.

Penmaenmawr shops at the turn of the century. At this time they were about twenty years old and well patronised. Pushing a handcart in the middle of the road is an 'outporter', who was hired to take luggage from the railway station to the residences of holidaying visitors.

(Courtesy Penmaenmawr Historical Society)

PENMAENMAWR.

The western end of Penmaenmawr, known as Penmaenan, around 1900. Improved jetties are in place and concrete hoppers of the Brundrit quarries, to facilitate the loading of railway wagons and ships, have been constructed.

(Courtesy Penmaenmawr Historical Society)

THE CHESTER
AND
HOLYHEAD RAILWAY

The station at Penmaenmawr owes its existence to the Chester and Holyhead Railway, engineered to link London with Dublin via a steam packet service operating from the port of Holyhead. The line opened in 1848 after the problems of crossing the River Conwy and Menai Strait into Anglesey had been solved by the engineer, Robert Stephenson, using tubular bridges. Tunnels were cut through the twin headlands of Penmaenbach and Penmaenmawr, which were further difficulties to be overcome; these major obstacles caused rival projects to be considered.....

By the 1830s a railway link to Dublin had been under serious consideration and in 1836 Commissioners were appointed to investigate a general system of railways in Ireland. They appointed Charles Vignoles as engineer and in March 1837 asked him to report, on investigations already made to connect railways on the English and Welsh side of the water. Vignoles was in favour of a railway through Barmouth, Bala and Llangollen to Porth Dynllaen near Caernarfon, rejecting a line from Chester to Holyhead because he felt that the engineering dificulties associated with crossing the Conwy and Menai Strait, as well as tunnelling problems through Penmaenbach and Penmaenmawr would be too great.

While the merits of these proposals to link London with Dublin were being considered, a third alternative was offered by the St. George's Harbour and Railway Company. This project envisaged a railway from Chester along the North Wales Coast to Ormes Bay, now Llandudno. This was eventually rejected because it was felt that people would rather go on by sea to Liverpool than stop at Ormes Head. While Vignoles pursued his case for a railway through Mid Wales to Port Dynllaen, Robert Stephenson had produced plans for overcoming the difficulties associated with engineering the line along the North Wales Coast. The main advantage of Holyhead lay in its established status as a packet station offering the shortest sea crossing to Ireland; moreover Chester was developing into a major railway junction having attracted, in the 1830s, the Chester and Birkenhead and Chester and Crewe Railways, opening their respective routes in 1840. It was these factors which finally convinced the authorities that the route along the North Wales Coast was the most suitable, compared with Vignoles' scheme, which would have required building a new port, and Royal Assent was given to the Chester and Holyhead Railway Bill on 4th July 1844.

The first signalbox erected at Penmaenmawr station, in a photograph of about 1880. In the background is the original fan of sidings serving the Darbishire Quarries whilst the grassland on the right would be taken up by further tracks in the next few years. On the left of the picture is the goods siding and shed built when the station first opened. The mountain beyond is Penmaenmawr, the site of the quarries; the station took its name, which was later adopted for the town.

(Courtesy Penmaenmawr Historical Society)

The LNWR considered Penmaenmawr important; enough to name one of its 'George V' 4-4-0s after the town, seen here as LMS No. 25392. Perhaps it is time that BR recognised this major source of stone traffic and named one of its own engines Penmaenmawr.

(Roger Carpenter Collection)

A late nineteenth century view of LNWR 2-2-2-2 compound locomotive, Greater Britain, east of Penmaenbach tunnel with a train for Llandudno Junction.

(A.G. Ellis Collection)

Once the railway was opened its economic impact upon the narrow coastal strip of North Wales was enormous. It brought in many summer visitors and the resident population increased to serve them until more than half of the inhabitants of Snowdonia came to be concentrated along a ribbon of land covering less than one eighth of its total area. While sea-bathing had been popular among the gentry and clergy from the end of the 18th century, many of them coming by their own gigs or stage coaches, it was the railway which brought the pleasures of the seaside to the masses, Penmaenmawr benefiting greatly in this new tourist 'boom'.

The railway also solved the long standing problem of passage into Penmaenmawr. Towards the middle years of the 19th century the road over Penmaenmawr mountain collapsed; this caused little stir as it was not much used but it rendered the village virtually inaccessible from Bangor in the west. When the line was built tunnels were cut through the headlands at great expense, and 20th century road builders followed this example by going round and under instead of over the headlands. Thus Penmaenmawr was now in a position

Ex LNWR 'Prince of Wales' 4-6-0 heads a train out of the western portal of Penmaenmawr tunnel c1934. Construction of a road tunnel linking Penmaenmawr to Llanfairfechan is underway
H.A.Coulter

to expand prodigiously from a small village into an important tourist town; the establishment of the station was vital to this development.

Had any of the other sites been chosen as ports to serve Ireland, then it is a distinct possibility that there would not have been a railway connection into Penmaenmawr. Developments at Chester would have prompted a line along the North Wales coast but engineering problems meant it would probably have only gone as far as Llandudno. Vignole's line was to have linked Bangor using Mid Wales and would have further isolated the village of Penmaenmawr. If this had occurred then the village may have remained very small, or would simply have faded away. The local quarrying industry may still have been served by ships, but this would not have been conducive to the innovatory work on crushed stone products for which Penmawnmawr is known, and if the trade for setts disappeared, then the quarries would surely have closed. The railway, therefore, was fundamental to the development of Penmaenmawr, as tourist and quarrying centre, and its growth into the small town we know today.

Unidentified 'Precursor' 4-4-0 leaves the western end of Penmaenmawr tunnel, crossing the viaduct on its way to Llanfairfechan with a train for Bangor, during the summer of 1934

(H.A.Coulter)

As the popularity of Penmaenmawr as a resort grew, a new road was cut to link the shopping centre with the railway station. Known, with some exaggeration, as Paradise Road, it was actually opened by William Gladstone in 1877, and was still relatively new when this photograph was taken.

EARLY DAYS AND INFLUENCES

Before the Chester and Holyhead Railway was built, Penmaenmawr was a tiny quarrying village in the parish of Dwygyfylchi. It was served by a turnpike road through the Sychnant Pass across the mountains, later replaced by a coast road engineered by Thomas Telford in 1825/6. The route through the village had always been dangerous because of road collapse, necessitating travel along the sea shore and the attendant risks of being caught by tides; on the road moreover it was possible to fall victim to highwaymen and thieves, who had preyed on travellers from early times. Those wishing to go to Bangor or Chester would seek to avoid the area if at all possible.

Even when the railway was planned and opened in 1848 there was no railway station here at Penmaenmawr - from Conwy there was to be no other station until the line reached Aber. A station *was* finally established in November 1849, at a cost of £500, in the space between the two headlands of Penmaenbach and Penmaenmawr, with only minimal pasenger facilities and a single siding on the down side with room for 16 wagons. Indeed so basic was it, that despite extensions added later, the platforms were not properly paved and the edges concreted until August 1888, at a cost of £106.

That a station should be established at all may have been due to a major figure in the town, Samuel Duckinfield Darbishire, who moved to Dwygyfylchi to play the part of the 'country squire' at Pendyffryn; he was, it is understood, a solicitor connected with the construction of the Chester and Holyhead Railway and was voted to the Board in March 1858. Darbishire liked Dwygyfylchi and this almost certainly influenced the establishment of the station, named after the mountain to the west of the village, *Penmaenmawr*, and the present name was first used in Bradshaw's Guide in the 1860s.

The name Penmaenmawr was chosen because it was felt the proper name of the village - Dwygyfylchi - would be unpronounceable. Such was the influence of the railway that the station name was eventually taken up as the name for the town and the original parish name now only exists in a small area to the east of the town.

The railway began to transform the local community and economy; the Victorian craze for sea bathing, considered healthy, helping to bring holidaymakers to the village. Once the station had been established the hope was that new property would arise round about, though this happened only slowly, wealthy people from Chester and Liverpool building holiday mansions above the station in the 1850s. By the end of that decade the present *Grand Hotel*, then called *The Penmaenmawr Hotel*, after the railway station, was built by a Dr. Norton. Such was its success that it was rebuilt twice and became *The Grand* after the second rebuild. From the 1860s there was further construction, all of which took place on the slopes above the railway station.

A major influence in the development of the town at this time was the patronage of William Ewart Gladstone, the Victorian Chancellor of the Exchequer and Prime Minister. He first visited Penmaenmawr in the late 1850s when introduced to the town by Darbishire, who had then bought Pendyffryn Hall, and who himself was a Liberal. Gladstone lived at Hawarden, near Chester, and so could join the train and be in Penmaenmawr in an hour. Penmaenmawr was still a quiet place in summer, so Gladstone would have come to rest from his labours. The wealthy and influential were holidaying in Penmaenmawr for fresh air, sea, peace and quiet and not for the sunshine - tanning was considered 'common' in Victorian society.

Penmaenmawr looking east around 1950, showing the jetties for the loading of ships. The nearest will close within the next five years. In the background is the headland of Penmaenbach, with the road tunnel just visible.

(Courtesy Mr.S. Buggins)

Gladstone usually came to Penmaenmawr in the autumn, staying at various houses in the town. On leaving in 1882 after a few weeks stay, he told the ever-present press that the 'health and strength which it had pleased God to give him during the past twenty years he owed in no small degree to the salubrity, fresh breezes and habits of life that prevail at Penmaenmawr'. That statement was well used by local hoteliers in publicising the town as a resort. These 'benefits' mentioned by Gladstone were influential in bringing many of the wealthy and famous into the town. Among those who came were composer Sir Edward Elgar, poet Alfred Lord Tennyson, naturalist and author of 'The Origin of Species' Charles Darwin and Queen Victoria's surgeon, Sir George Paget.

Four times Prime Minister, William Ewart Gladstone, with his wife. It was Gladstone who popularised Penmaenmawr, to the benefit of the railway and station, remarking upon its value as a place for fresh air, peace and quiet in his many speeches. A statue dedicated to him was erected in the town but the bronze bust was stolen in 1979, never to be recovered.

(Courtesy Gwynedd Archive)

Between 1850 and 1890 Penmaenmawr became quite a place on the tourist map, and many guide books of the day made a point of the 'sea air' and 'glorious views', as well as the easy access to the town by rail. Most of the visitors came to the town by rail, whereas travellers to Llandudno, Beaumaris, Bangor and Caernarfon were still arriving by paddle steamer from Liverpool. To cope with this increase in traffic, the station was rebuilt in 1865 and extended in 1868/9 and 1877.

Apartment houses were built for the middle and upper classes, many by skilled local quarrymen who set up their wives as housekeepers. When the lodging houses were built new shops were put up in the centre of Penmaenmawr above the railway station, where the shopping area remains today. The old shopping streets had been further west, under the quarry. In 1895 a road was built, and actually officially opened by Gladstone, to link the new shops with the railway station, some 45 years after it opened. Prior to this the only road from the station ran parallel with the railway east to west. *Station Road* went directly to the *Penmaenmawr (Grand) Hotel.*

Like many stations Penmaenmawr greatly influenced the development of the local community and economy. Without it the tourist trade may not have become the major force it did, or its development must certainly have been slower. The town remained an important tourist haunt until the early 1960s, with the station a necessary part.

The railway was of particular importance during the two World Wars. There was indeed a direct link between Liverpool, Manchester, London and Penmaenmawr which allowed the army to establish training camps away from the centres of enemy action; during World War One there was a prisoner-of-war camp at Graiglwyd Hall, allowing for easy control of the prisoners and the only way to bring them in was by rail.

The Second World War brought evacuee children from the major cities of Liverpool, Manchester and Birmingham and even during the hostilities Penmaenmawr thrived as a holiday centre, the war weary escaping the stresses of the cities. Such were the numbers coming in that there were complaints of food shortages. Government Ministries had offices in *The Grand Hotel* for the duration, all of them served by the railway and the station.

Erasmus Street, **Penmaenmawr, an example of terraced housing built by the Darbishire Company for its quarrymen.**

(Courtesy Mrs E.A.Hitches)

Penmaenan, from the original Brundrit Quarry, showing terraced houses built by the Brundrit Company for their employees. In the background is Penmaenmawr town, the railway station, granite sidings, hoppers, part of the jetty and the promenade.

(J.Hefin Jones)

*Graiglwyd Hall, **Penmaenmawr**. It was used as a prisoner of war camp during World War One and German captives were put to work in the quarry, in place of locals serving in the forces. During the Second World War the hall became a school, for children evacuated from Kent.*

(Courtesy Mrs Wendy Williams)

A photograph from the Darbishire family album, the bridge over the main line which carried the quarry railway to the sidings and the then small jetty for loading ships. The quarry railway is under construction in this view of 1879
(Courtesy University College of North Wales, Bangor)

A similarly faded photograph from the same album, showing the original fan of sidings from the western end, around 1879.
(Courtesy University College of North Wales, Bangor)

Braichllwyd Mill, the first stone crushing mill built by the Darbishire Company, in 1888, to produce railway ballast for the London & North Western Railway. The LNWR placed an initial order for 500,000 tons of granite ballast, at three shillings (15p) a ton, in 1888, followed by orders for a further 1,000,000 tons in 1893 and another 1,250,000 tons in 1899, to replace cinder ballast then in use all over their system. Another major contract was awarded to Penmaenmawr following the Grouping of 1923, when the LMS ordered granite ballast to bring the old Lancashire and Yorkshire Railway track up to LNWR standards.
(Courtesy Penmaenmawr Historical Society)

THE QUARRIES AND DEVELOPMENT OF THE SIDINGS

Quarrying of granite at Dwygyfylchi commenced in 1830 when the Brundrit and Whiteway Company of Runcorn opened a quarry on the western side of Penmaenmawr mountain, to produce stone setts, the blocks we now call cobblestones, for use in the the new tramways then appearing in towns and cities throughout Britain. The stone chippings left after the setts were dressed and shaped were sold as Macadam for road surfaces.

Expansion of the sett and Macadam production was possible when a new quarry opened on the eastern side of the mountain, through the partnership of Brassey and Tomkinson, in 1834. The Brassey member of the partnership was Thomas, the contractor involved in the building of the London and Southampton Railway who had financed a line between Godalming and Portsmouth. The quarry was sold to the Kneeshaw, Raynes and Lupton partnership in 1840. Virtually all the products of these workings left Penmaenmawr by sea from jetties built by the quarry owners, to Liverpool and Chester to reach their final destinations by road or canal.

C.H.Darbishire, the man responsible for bringing mechanical stone crushing to Penmaenmawr; this allowed the production of railway ballast so important to the railway and to the economy of the town.
(Courtesy Gwynedd Archive)

First step to get the stone moving by rail was born out of necessity, when the Graiglwyd Quarry was bought from the Kneeshaw partnership by the Darbishire family in 1878. Not only had the Kneeshaws removed all plant and equipment from the site but they still held the lease from the Crown for use of the jetty, and this did not expire until 1887. Thus the new proprietors were not able to use ships and were forced to turn to the railway. For the first ten years, Darbishire Quarries sent much of their stone sett production by rail to Cei'r-Ynys wharf in Conwy on the Llandudno Junction side of the tubular bridge, where they were loaded on to vessels of the St. George's Shipping Company for removal to their final destinations. At the same time, further expansion of British tramways meant greater demand for stone setts, one large order for Belfast going by rail to Connah's Quay, near Flint.

Having proved that the railway could handle this traffic, by 1879 most of Darbishire's stone was going by rail, to destinations along the North Wales coast and as afar afield as Huddersfield, Leeds, Manchester, Warrington, Oldham and Birmingham. Stone was even going to Chester and Liverpool by rail, successfully competing with ships carrying products from the Brundrit Company. Broken stone - Macadam and 'Breakers', a rough stone used as hardcore under road surfaces, were all being sent by rail.

The sidings were considerably expanded during the later years of the nineteenth century as greater provision was made for transferring stone from the narrow gauge wagons of the quarry to the standard gauge of the national system. Further developments occurred when Darbishire started to experiment with mechanical stone crushing. There was an increasing demand for Macadam as new roads developed and in 1881 he visited a quarry in Leicestershire to see a stone crushing mill, which had been installed there in 1867. This was followed by a visit to Clitheroe in 1882 to see a jaw type crusher used on hard limestone. Two years later a new crusher was bought for the Graiglwyd Quarry and put to use for a new road then being built for the new booming tourist trade in Penmaenmawr.

Proving the success of mechanical stone crushing, a start was made in 1888 on the construction of a crushing mill at Braichllwyd, to produce railway ballast for the London and North Western Railway. According to Permanent Way Superintendents T. Brocklebank and W. Brocklehurst in their report to the Board on 19th June 1889, *ballasting with crushed granite is economical and advantageous to the preservation of rails, chairs and sleepers,* thus assuring the future of granite as a suitable material. The economics of the Darbishire quarry, producing ballast alongside stone setts and Macadam was also a consideration and the fact that the Northern Division of the LNWR was spending an average of £1,400 per month on track ballasting in 1888 suggested that it was worthwhile investing in Braichllwyd Mill. It was duly completed and the first train load of ballast left the sidings, with all due ceremony, on 15th August 1889; there has been at least one ballast train leaving Penmaenmawr every working day since.

By the time the lease which precluded the Darbishire Company use of the jetty had expired, the movement of stone by rail had become firmly established and production from the quarry was also changing, making for greater emphasis on rail borne traffic. Although ships did call at the jetty fairly regularly, movement of stone by sea was never so important for Darbishire.

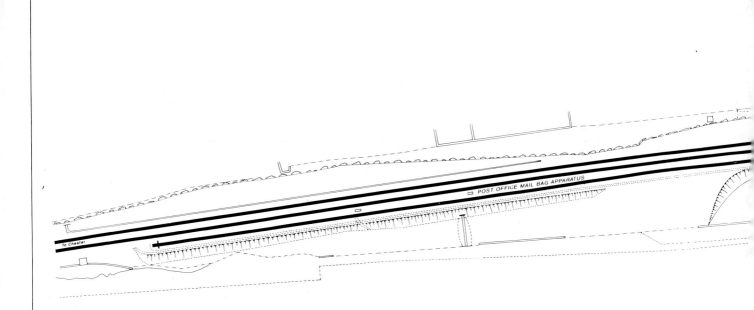

To Chester

POST OFFICE MAIL BAG APPARATUS

L & N W R – P E N M A E N M A W R   1 8 9 5

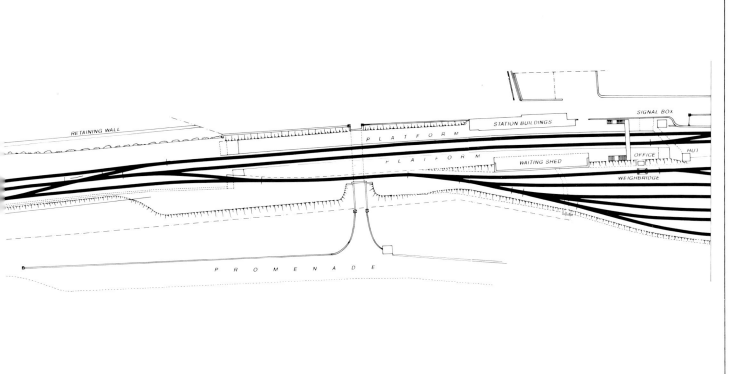

RETAINING WALL

P L A T F O R M

P L A T F O R M

STATION BUILDINGS

SIGNAL BOX

WAITING SHED

OFFICE

HUT

WEIGHBRIDGE

P R O M E N A D E

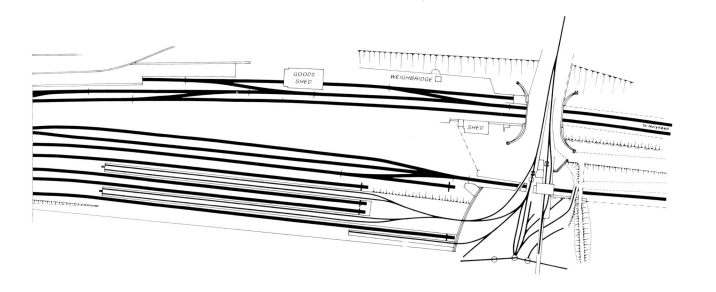

GOODS SHED

WEIGHBRIDGE

SHED

To Holyhead

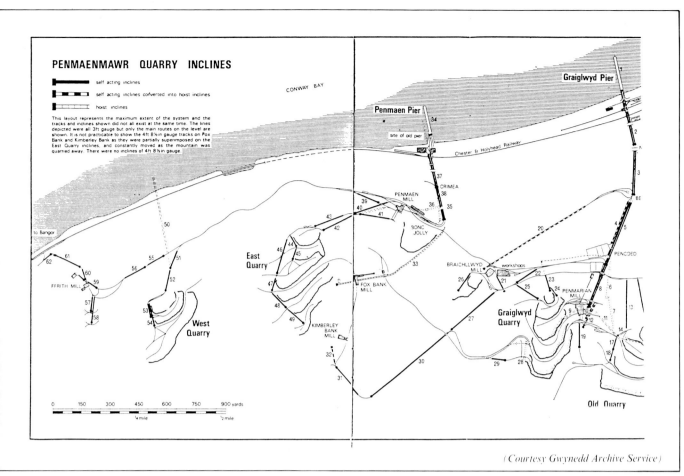

(Courtesy Gwynedd Archive Service)

The Penmarian Mill of the Darbishire Quarry. This was the second stone crushing mill, built to meet increasing demand.

(Courtesy Penmaenmawr Historical Society)

There were also changes at the Penmaen Quarry of the Brundrit Company; a stone crushing mill of a similar design to that at Graiglwyd was constructed and this went into operation on 13th August 1893, producing crushed stone in competition with Darbishire. The Penmaen Quarry Company had their own yard known as 'Wright's Sidings', a little further west of the station and even their own railway wagons, but they never became as important as those of Darbishire, and were never extended, athough they were still in use in 1952.

Over the years the stone taken from the quarries was removed more and more by train and hoppers were eventually built between the railway sidings and the jetty in order to facilitate the loading of wagons. The hoppers were fed by belts which would ensure that the LNWR 20 ton ballast wagons could be loaded at a rate of 700 tons per hour; there is still between 150,000 to 2000,000 tons of railway ballast sent away annually.

The development of the sidings at Penmaenmawr station derived solely from the quarry industry. Spurred initially through the prohibition on shipping rights, they became very important as production changed from setts to crushed stone, at first for ballast and then for cement products and roadstone. Had the right to use ships from the jetty existed from the start, then the sidings might not have developed so early. Stone crushing had been considered by Darbishire from the time he bought the Graiglwyd Quarry, for road Macadam, and railway ballast was a progression from this. Once the stone was purchased as track ballast the LNWR naturally carried it in its own trains; the sidings developed from that point.

The railway nevertheless did not acquire a monopoly of the traffic. There was the initial competition from ships, which continued (albeit much reduced) until the early 1970s, when the jetties were finally closed. Today the main, and most serious competitor is the lorry, and in recent years the station sidings have been much reduced in size; most traffic leaving the station yard nowadays is ballast for British Rail.

The bottom of the main incline with the quarry office, some of the company wagons and a horizontal boilered locomotive in the background. Below are the Darbishire sidings around 1900, showing the storage hoppers and pier for the loading of ships.
(*Courtesy Penmaenmawr Historical Society*)

The sidings serving Darbishire Quarry traffic as they were in 1905, looking east. The growth of these sidings has begun to dwarf the station. Visible on the right of the picture is the LNWR signalbox, replacing the original which nevertheless remains in situ, used as a storeroom.

Courtesy Penmaenmawr Historical Society)

The station in 1877, shortly after the final extensions were made to the buildings, perhaps the earliest existing picture of the station. Although the building 'boom' is not apparent by this date, the 'bathing machines', people on the promenade and the already established Penmaenmawr Hotel on the left of the picture, indicate that the village is already becoming popular as a resort. The lack of shipping at the jetty is evidence of Darbishire's exclusion from it; this explains why the land between the station and promenade would be filled with railway tracks within the next twenty years, expanding to meet the increasing demand for the stone won from the mountain above.

(Courtesy Penmaenmawr Historical Society)

Twenty one years on the building boom is well underway and new houses are awaiting their roofs on Marine Terrace. The station has now been signalled with Saxby and Farmer equipment, the platform has been properly paved, and the quarry sidings have had their first extension. In the background the new Darbishire Jetty is complete.

(Roger Carpenter Collection)

NINETEENTH CENTURY
DEVELOPMENTS
IN AND AROUND THE STATION

The present station building on the down platform dates from 1868 and although not designed by the Chester and Holyhead Railway architect, Francis Thompson, has similarities to many of his other stations. Extensions and alterations were made in 1877, including a large waiting shelter on the up platform; it was demolished in 1970 and replaced by the bus shelter type waiting area still in use. The station was originally supplied with a small goods siding when opened in 1849. With increases in traffic another was established at Pendyffryn, 1½ miles east of the station in 1857/8, but it was the development of the stone traffic from 1888 which prompted significant extension of the sidings.

There have been three different signal boxes. The first was sited on the up platform and was replaced by one of early LNWR type on the opposite platform; both were situated at the Bangor end behind the footbridge, built in 1884. The current signal box was built in 1953 and stands at the Chester end of the down platform, an experimental 'system' designed forerunner of the British Railways standard box and an outcome of the Penmaenmawr accident of 1950.

When the station opened in 1849 the service was already established with five trains each way every day between Chester and Bangor, comprising a morning 'Irish Mail', an afternoon express and three stopping trains - one each in the morning, afternoon and evening. Opening of the line over the Menai Bridge in March 1850 caused the introduction of a new timetable with three expresses, one morning and one evening 'Irish Mail' and a morning 'Irish Boat Express' from Euston, with corresponding workings from Holyhead.

Local services continued much as before but with a Parliamentary train, so called through *The Regulation of the Railways Act 1844*, which stipulated that at least one train a day in each direction should carry covered third class accommodation at a fare of not more than one penny per mile, travelling at not less than 12 mph, running the full length of the line in each direction. There were also additional stopping trains between Chester and Bangor. The company tried several alterations to these trains during this period, so the station would have been fairly busy from the start.

Penmaenmawr.

At the turn of the century new building was more or less at an end, as this winter view indicates. The granite sidings had expanded still further, with the headshunt now in place and land between the station and promenade now part of the sidings complex

(Courtesy Mrs. Wendy Williams)

Penmaenmawr station from the promenade c.1900. The back of the waiting shelter is visible along with the old Chester and Holyhead Railway signalbox, the replacement LNWR box and the footbridge. A stone wagon can be seen in the foreground at the sidings. This view is no longer possible for the promenade has gone, replaced by a new structure, the first in Britain since Victorian times, making way for the A55 Expressway. It now divides the railway station from the promenade and is screened by slabs of concrete.

(Courtesy Penmaenmawr Historical Society)

Between 1855 and 1860 there were approximately ten trains each way every day in the summer including the Mails and expresses and eight in the winter, with four trains a day on Sundays throughout the year. In 1849 there were two daily goods each way to Bangor and Chester and traffic steadily increased as more went by rail rather than by sea. In 1852 a fish service started from Dublin to Manchester. Other traffic included oysters from Caernarfon and slate; by 1853 1,000 tons per week went by rail.

When the station first opened there was little in the way of signalling for the 'time interval' system , which simply allowed trains a given time to clear sections, was generally in use on the Chester to Holyhead Railway. Accidents at Rhyl and Abergele through signalling shortcomings and confusion deriving from time interval practice prompted the LNWR to make substantial improvements. By February 1867 all signals had to correspond with those used on the rest of the LNWR system and in September of that year an agreement was reached with Messrs Saxby and Farmer to supply brick signal cabins, junction and station semaphores on 25ft posts either in wood or wrought iron, plus point and signal lever apparatus, as well as all the necessary ancillary equipment. Penmaenmawr received its first signal box by the mid-1870s and this was placed on the up platform.

The telegraph was the main device for safety improvements on the railway and was first used in tunnels on the Chester and Holyhead. Penmaenbach tunnel was so protected by 1859, with the wooden huts built to work the telegraph replaced by brick structures some five years later, perhaps as a precaution against rock falls. The block telegraph system was ordered for the whole of the Chester and Holyhead line by February 1869.

It was still crude but by October 1870 the 'absolute block' (inherently safer) was ordered and by 1872 the 'speaking telegraph' was installed throughout, with re-arrangement of the station signals and siting further back of distant signals where appropriate by 1872. In November 1871 a ruling was made that all points and signals should be interlocked. Safety thus advanced immensely in the 1870s and Penmaenmawr station benefitted from many of these improvements. This would become increasingly important as stone output from the quarries rose and traffic increased.

Rails used on the Chester and Holyhead were primarily iron, until 1876 when Francis Webb (the LNWR Chief Mechanical Engineer) ordered bull-headed steel rail on all main lines and 84lb rail (the weight per yard) in sidings. Until this time rail lengths were 30ft. and were only replaced (individually) where necessary; that there were few accidents with this type of rail was largely due to the lower speeds of the period.

Other improvements were made in the mid-nineteenth century, including an overbridge, built in 1879 and 1880 to carry the stone traffic *over* the railway, supplanting the existing (and obviously inconvenient) level crossing. Another bridge built at Penmaenbach in the same year was to give access to a brick works owned by Darbishire. In 1855 the sea wall was strengthened with further work carried out in 1860 after severe storm damage. By the 1870s the station had become firmly established with good accommodation; it was well signalled and enjoyed good sea defences and was ready to benefit from burgeoning passenger and freight traffic.

The necessity placed upon the Darbishire quarries to move stone by rail rendered the existing sidings at Penmaenmawr

The Promenade, Penmaenmawr.

Brundrit sidings around 1898, showing the bridge over the main line, the stone tramway from the quarry face to the jetty and railway. This spot is now hidden by a huge concrete bridge carrying the A55 expressway from the site of the old promenade up to Llanfairfechan.

(Roger Carpenter Collection)

inadequate and they were extended by the mid 1870s. The entrance to these lay to the west of the station and in order to cope with the extra traffic the LNWR built a new signal box on the down platform in the 1880s. The original box was decommissioned and used as a store for the station. While the new signalbox (as we have seen) lasted until 1953, when it was replaced by one at the Chester end of the station, the original was still in use for storage until finally demolished in 1970.

The rapid expansion of the Darbishire quarries into crushed stone products notably ballast, led inevitably to demands for further sidings. In 1892 plans were drawn up to replace the existing lines with a new arrangement, a single line connection from the sidings to the main line at the Chester end of the station. When these were laid the original small fan of sidings was lifted and the area landscaped. These new sidings allowed for interchange with the narrow gauge railway of the quarry company, making the loading of main line wagons so much easier and the transfer of stone much more rapid.

There were further developments in the expansion of the sidings at the turn of the century; plans were drawn up in 1895 for a headshunt from the points where the sidings joined the main line, to go some distance to the east of the station and, in the process, the mail pick-up apparatus was to be moved a short distance along the track towards Conwy. This headshunt was constructed by the end of the century and its basic layout is still in existence.

To the west of the sidings used by Darbishire Quarries and

beyond the overbridge carrying the quarry railway over the main line were the much smaller sidings of the Brundrit Quarry. These were made up of three tracks, linked to the main line close by the overbridge. The Brundrit sidings were smaller because the Co. already had a well established jetty for shipping out products by sea and they only needed sidings for crushed stone produced in competition with Darbishire. Darbishire, on the other hand, had been forced to use the railways much earlier.

Between the 1870s and the end of the century, Penmaenmawr had begun to benefit from the new tourist trade and to make the town even more attractive to visitors a promenade was built in the 1880s, connected to the road by the existing subway, cut under the station to the east. The rapid increase in tourism, along with the success of the quarries, brought brighter employment prospects and the population increased accordingly. Between 1850 and 1900 it rose by 2,577, all of them attracted by the new opportunities.

Increases in passenger traffic during the summer months helped to develop and expand the tourist trade in the town. Excursion trains were popular with the 'working classes'; they were frequently used elsewhere along the North Wales coast but did not visit Penmaenmawr until the early part of this century, after the local Council requested that such trains should come to the town. Thus Penmaenmawr was a rather *elitist* place in the nineteenth century, a preserve of the upper and middle classes.

The Penmaen Quarry of the Brundrit Company, west of the station, had no problems in the use of their jetty, evident in this view of a ship awaiting its cargo of stone around 1880. This explains why the railway sidings were never expanded here in the same way as they were behind the station.

(Courtesy Penmaenmawr Historical Society)

The mail pick-up apparatus on the up main line, just east of the station. About 1880.
(Courtesy Penmaenmawr Historical Society)

Mail equipment on the down main line, east of the station, again about 1880.

(Courtesy Penmaenmawr Historical Society)

Extract from 1911 O.S.Sheet. Crown Copyright Reserved

THE QUARRY RAILWAYS

Narrow gauge railways were established in the quarries through the need to remove stone setts from the works high up on the mountain to the jetties for loading on to ships for such places as Runcorn, where they would then go by canal to other parts of the country. The first lines were cable worked, the full wagons lowered down the mountain and empties winched back up. By the 1870s with increased demand the first steam locomotive, the *Mona* was used in the Penmaen quarry to haul stone from the West quarry to Bonc Jolly. *Mona* was not a great success and was superseded in 1878 by *Penmaen*, built by the De Winton Company of Caernarfon and used for the next seventy years on the steep face of the mountain above the main A55 road.

When the Darbishires took over the Graiglwyd quarries in 1878 from the Kneeshaw partners, all the railway track and winding gear consisting of three inclines to connect the workings with the jetty and railway sidings had been removed. Fortunately C.H. Darbishire became manager of the new quarry and he was a good civil engineer with experience of railway construction in Great Britain and in Italy as well as in the Penyrorsedd slate quarry in Nantlle. The new layout had four inclines instead of the previous three which increased the speed of transit, particularly important as four new sett banks, eventually increased to six, were opened at Nant Dywyll.

The lease which precluded the use of the jetties for the Darbishires expired in 1887 and a new jetty was opened on 23rd June the following year. The level of the quay was raised by 25 feet at this time and this allowed the railway tracks on the jetty to run at a gradient, as a self acting incline.

The advent of stone crushing to supply railway ballast and the opening of the Braichllwyd mill meant that a way had to be found to move the product to the main line. An incline of 640

A train of stone from Brundrit West Quarry runs around the mountainside, headed by a horizontal boilered locomotive.
(Courtesy Penmaenmawr Historical Society)

yards was made leading to the parking sidings behind Ty Mawr. At first a horse was used to haul the wagons from the parking sidings but in 1891 the first vertical boilered engine, *Lilian* supplied by De Winton of Caernarfon did the work. Soon afterwards four more of these locomotives were operating in other areas of the quarry. These were followed later by four horizontal boilered locomotives from the Hunslet Engine Company.

Following construction of the jetty, quays were built which allowed 160 railway wagons alongside. The little vertical boilered locomotives nicknamed 'coffee-pots' were much used for running these wagons along the sidings. The quarry lines ran on 3ft gauge. A standard gauge track with space for 80 main line ballast wagons was laid with a slight gradient so that they would run to be filled under a ballast hopper. In 1900 a wooden ballast hopper holding 3,000 tons was erected in line with the jetty with an elevated trackway leading to it for the storage of stone ready for shipment. The quarry companies built their own wagons for the narrow gauge; usually of two ton capacity they eventually numbered several hundred. In 1911 the quarry companies in Penmaenmawr were amalgamated with the Welsh Granite Company of Trefor to form the Penmaenmawr and Welsh Granite Company and, in 1912, a rail link was built between Bonc Jolly of the old Brundrit Quarry and the Braichllwyd of the old Darbishire Company. A new jetty was built in 1913 for the Penmaen Quarry and this had two parallel self-acting inclines with a new concrete hopper of 3,000 tons capacity built the following year. A similar jetty, greater in length and double the width of the previous one, was built for the Graiglwyd Quarry.

By 1931 the Braichllwyd incline was converted to a single track haulage way and a hoist track was built leading up the mountainside from Bonc Jolly to the Kimberley floor, a lift of over 800 feet and a gradient of 1 in 1½ in part. The winding drum was powered by a 120 horse power motor.

The Kimberley level received in the same year two standard gauge diesel locomotives built by Avonside and, in 1934, an ex-Lancashire and Yorkshire Railway 0-4-0 saddle tank engine No. 43 which had been on dock working, probably at Goole. This engine was used as a stand-by in case of failure of the diesel locomotives. The Avonside company also supplied a 3 foot gauge, 74 horse power, diesel electric locomotive to haul stone from first crushing to the Penmarian Mill. By 1932 loading of stone was performed by mechanical shovel into standard gauge iron wagons, which were hauled to the crushers by the Avonside diesel locomotives but in 1949 this was done by specially designed lorries, eliminating the expense of frequently moving and extending the railway track. From the primary crusher the stone fell into an open bunker and was then hauled in 3 ton wagons by an 80 horse power diesel engine to the Penmarian Mill where the wagons were discharged two at a time by an electrically operated tipper. From here the crushed stone passed down a chute and, by the 1950s, by belt to the hoppers for transport by road or rail.

When lorries and conveyor belts were introduced from the 1950s the quarry railways went out of use. From the 1870s when the first steam locomotive was introduced, there have been 27 locomotives (steam, diesel and petrol) hauling over 400 two ton wagons of 3 feet gauge and 8 diesel and one steam locomotive of standard gauge, used on the lines. These railways were very important in connecting the workings, both with the jetties to move stone by sea, and, of later importance, moving stone to the sidings at Penmaenmawr railway station.

An example of the vertical boilered steam locomotives built by DeWinton of Caernarfon, known locally as 'Coffee Pots' and used extensively in the quarries and within the sidings at the station.

(Courtesy University College of North Wales, Bangor)

The last DeWinton 'Coffee Pot' of the Darbishire Co. awaits its fate at the west end of the granite sidings on 16th March 1963. It was eventually bought privately and is now preserved at Penrhyn Castle, Bangor. To the left are two of the wagons used on the quarry face itself.

(Keith Smith)

INTO THE TWENTIETH CENTURY

The tourist trade continued to flourish during the early years of the twentieth century, the railway having a virtual monopoly on bringing visitors into the town. Road competition was almost non-existent and the only real alternative to the railways was still the horse and cart. In order to cope with the increasing tourist trade, the railway company put on many extra trains during the summer, both to stop at Penmaenmawr station and to pass through for destinations west of the town. The great number of passengers made for a large station staff as well as those required for duties in the goods sidings. By 1914 there were no less than fourteen, including a stationmaster. Compare this with the 1980s when there was only one on duty at any time when the station was open, and no stationmaster. From October 1987 the station indeed became an unmanned halt.

The demand for crushed stone products led the Darbishire quarries to build a new stone crushing mill in 1900 and this started work in 1902, producing 700 to 800 tons a day. The Brundrit Company also built a duplicate mill in 1900 in response to increasing demand for these products. Most left Penmaenmawr by rail. The demand for stone setts had faded by 1908 and eventually all products from the quarries were crushed stone. The falling off of sett orders did not prevent the quarries from working to full capacity throughout the first decade of the 20th century, employing in excess of 1,000 men.

The Darbishire and Brundrit Companies were merged in 1911 and this allowed further developments when a tarmacadam plant was established in 1912. The stone from the Penmaen quarry was used for this process as it absorbed tar oils better than that from the Darbishire Quarries. The tar mill was established on the Graiglwyd quay of the old Darbishire quarries for this process and the coated results moved only by rail.

At the outbreak of the First World War in 1914 the town was quite prosperous, with full employment at the quarries and plenty of business coming from the thriving tourist trade. The railway and the station which had played a major part in this came under the control of the Government when war broke out in August 1914. The strategic importance of the railways was well understood and though the new Railway Executive Committee discouraged passenger traffic for civilians this had little effect. Even though most restaurant cars disappeared from main express trains and by 1917 cheap fares were abolished, ordinary fares rose by 50% and train services were drastically cut, many people still travelled and took seaside holidays, much to the benefit of Penmaenmawr.

Many of the quarrymen of the town volunteered for army services when war broke out, mostly for service in France. C.H. Darbishire was asked to form a 'Quarry Battalion' to serve behind the lines. Most of the men in the battalion were the older quarrymen. In the ensuing slaughter some 72 of them were killed.

The loss of so many men to the armed services left a depleted labour force and pressure on demand for the products needed for the war effort. In 1917 this problem was partly solved by using German prisoners-of-war, brought to Graiglwyd Hall by train to quarry the required stone. The railway still brought in the visitors, despite the wishes of the Railway Executive and the products of the quarry were still sent away, mostly by rail, much as before. The end of the war, however, brought with it an uncertain future and some changes which would have long term effects on the railway. The First World War had accelerated the development of motor transport and created men who were skilled enough to drive and maintain these vehicles. Many of them, on leaving the armed forces, started their own haulage businesses; others were absorbed into the new expanding bus and coach industry and this created a new and severe form of competition for the railways. The effects of this new development on the railway at Penmaenmawr would become apparent in later years.

The station staff, 1914. Their number indicates the importance of the railway as a local employer. The quantity of luggage is a measure of the popularity of Penmaenmawr as a tourist centre.
(Cty Penmaenmawr Historical Society)

Ex-LNWR 'Claughton' 4-6-0 passes the old LNWR signalbox, whistling its departure from Penmaenmawr with a local train for Bangor.

(A.G.Ellis Collection)

A view from the footbridge, towards the west, in 1935. The main line to Holyhead is on the left, the goods shed left of that. To the right are the granite sidings with hoppers in the background. A train of loaded ballast wagons is awaiting departure. The original signalbox is in the centre, then in use as a storeroom. It was demolished in 1970.

(Courtesy of Clwyd Record Office)

INTER WAR YEARS

The years after the First World War were marked by industrial unrest and Depression, both of which had an effect on the railway. The first serious competition from the motor vehicle occurred around this time, and the railways were forced to make changes in order to meet this challenge. The Government continued its control of the railways until 15th August 1921 and paid compensation for abnormal maintenance costs incurred as a result of wartime traffic. This compensation was slow in coming but eventually £60 million was allocated. Demands for the railways to be nationalised had been heard during the War and there were advantages in standardisation but politically the Government was opposed to it during peacetime, envisaging wholesale amalgamation instead. It was this idea which was embodied in *The Railways Act* of 1921. The Act called for the 120 companies to be organised into four Groups, to take effect on 1st January 1923. The London and North Western Railway, along with others including the Midland Railway and the Lancashire and Yorkshire Railway which had already merged with the LNWR in anticipation of changes to come, became the London, Midland and Scottish Railway and Penmaenmawer station became part of this giant new concern.

Ex-LNWR 'Experiment' class 4-6-0 No. 5472 approaches the western portal of Penmaenmawr tunnel c.1934. The cranes to the left are for the Pen-Y-Clip contract to improve the North Wales Coast road and, in consequence, bring severe competition to the railway.

(H.A. Coulter)

Industrial unrest, which had been festering since before the outbreak of war, broke out on the railway with the national rail strike of 1919 bringing the network to a standstill. This strike allowed the development of competition from the roads as travellers looked for alternatives to trains. Motor coaches proved attractive as they offered door to door service at lower prices, which more than made up for longer journey times. The immediate post war years also brought a boom in demand for private motor cars and Morris Motors increased car production from 3,076 in 1921 to 55,582 in 1925. This was done by cutting the cost of buying a car and demand began to increase. In 1922 the Austin Seven appeared, the first 'mini' family car and this began the age of mass motoring. To accommodate the increase in road transport, schemes to improve the country's roads were introduced. The road through Penmaenmawr was so dealt with in 1934 with tunnels through Penmaenbach and Penmaenmawr.

Despite the economic depression passenger travel by land transport in Britain increased by 48% between 1920 and 1938 but most of this was attributable to private or public road vehicles. In order to compete with the expansion of road transport, the railway companies offered cheaper fares and better accommodation. There were special excursion trains, both full day and half day trips, with very low fares. Low fares were also introduced on long distance trains and scheduled services including such things as three day tickets at single fare. The LMS also introduced 'Save to Travel' in 1936, a scheme which offered interest of a halfpenny a month for a year on every ten shillings saved. By 1938 around 85% of passenger receipts were derived from reduced fares compared with 34.4% in 1924. The effect of all this was that average receipts per passenger mile fell from 0.86 pence to 0.67 pence in the same period.

The incentive schemes provided by the railways ensured that the majority of visitors to Penmaenmawr still came by train, but others were now coming by private car. The long distance motor coach was in its infancy during this period and very few tourists would have come to the town in this way. They would, however, have used local buses to visit the various places of interest rather than the railway, although reduced fares would have lured some onto the train. Thus the station remained a very busy place during these years.

Business in the quarries continued to be buoyant immediately after the First World War. The tar coating plant was still very active and plans were made in 1920 to extend the sidings still further for another 34 wagons, build a new hopper and establish tar tanks on the site. A subsidiary company, The Penmaenmawr and Trinidad Lake Asphalt Company Limited, was established in 1921 for this business. This company undertook road laying with its asphalt, a sign of things to come. All of the tar products left by rail initially but as lorries became more established it gradually began to go by road.

A new hopper of 7,000 tons capacity was constructed in 1922/3 at Penmaen Quay just west of an earlier construction, increasing rail traffic still further. This demand for stone ensured that the quarries remained a major employer during the 1920s with manpower at a peak of 1100. There was, however, change on the way which would reduce the workforce substantially......

The demands of the First World War had left the LNWR short of wagons suitable for removing stone products, leaving the quarry company with transport difficulties. In an effort to resolve this problem, the company bought 270 new ten ton wooden plank wagons, in 1920, suitable for stone haulage, supplementing a hundred that had been bought in 1912, and 60 second hand coal wagons, built in 1895. All of these wagons were lettered 'Penmaenmawr & Welsh Granite Co.'. The coal wagons proved unsuitable for stone traffic and they went on indefinite loan to the LNER in 1939. When wagons were not required by the quarry company, they were leased to other firms ensuring that the Company's investment remained profitable.

By 1931 demand for setts virtually disappeared, for roads by now were more or less universally tarmacked, for the pneumatic tyre. Along with this came the Great Depression which led to a collapse of demand for crushed stone. The result was that 100 men were laid off in 1930 with a further 560 in 1932 and before the end of the year the total labour force was only 388. The only production from the quarries was crushed stone and this at a time when there was competiton from natural washed and screened gravel, often available near to where it was required. Penmaenmawr stone is extremely hard (a fine grained, closely packed and very enduring variety of granite) and was only reduced to marketable size with great difficulty; the only way to compete was through greater mechanisation and the management decided to move in that direction. After a visit to the United States of America a change of method was decided upon which would allow for the stone to be broken up by machinery with almost no involvement from the workforce. The consequence was that employment fell still further and there was no demand for skilled labour.

The changing production methods in the quarries meant that in terms of employment the tourist industry was now preeminent with a consequent decline in living standards. Most of those in tourism were women whose income could not match earnings in quarrying.

Many of the men laid off during the rationalisation in the quarries found work on the new road development. Such work was sponsored in the late 1930s by the Government, in order to reduce the effects of unemployment which by an unfortunate consequence aided competition from the roads.

The Depression and unemployment of the 1930s was only alleviated by the outbreak of World War Two and the railway would then become increasingly important, serving the town as well as it had done in the past.

A 1920s view of the eastern end of Penmaenmawr station with a train purporting to be 'The Welshman'. It is in fact a local headed by an LMS 0-6-0. The gas lighting was due to be renewed at this time and the local council wrote to the LMS suggesting that they use electricity, to match that being installed in the town. The railway company declined and electric lights did not appear until 1970.

(Courtesy Clwyd Record Office)

ACCIDENTS AND NEAR MISSES

Accidents in and around Penmaenmawr have occurred at various times over the years since the station opened. The first of note occurred on 10th April 1854, when a train shunting at Wright's siding, ¾ mile west of the station, and used for loading stone setts, left six wagons on the up main line. These were run into by the 6pm passenger train from Bangor and one passenger was injured.

The accident was caused through a preceding argument amongst various officials, concerning orders given to the brakesman. These had been verbal only and were at variance with other instructions given to a goods foreman at Conwy. These arguments delayed the 1.15pm goods from Chester which arrived at Penmaenmawr 1 hour and 9 minutes late and commenced shunting when the passenger train was due.

The siding had distant signals in each direction but these were under the control of the agent for the quarry owners and not the railway company. Before shunting started, the lever for the up line distant was set to danger but the wire had become slack and the signal did not respond. Even if the signal had been set to danger, the passenger train could not have stopped; it was only three minutes away when shunting commenced and the driver's view was obstructed until the last moment by the Penmaenmawr tunnel. The Chester and Holyhead Railway Traffic Committee immediately put a man in charge of the signals and his wages were paid by the quarry owners.

High winds and storms have long been a problem in winter and frequently assail the Penmaenmawr section of the North Wales coast. When these coincide with a very high tide, then heavy seas with waves of great strength break against the shore and can create much damage. Precisely such conditions conspired to bring about the disaster at Penmaenbach tunnel on the night of Thursday 12th January 1899.....

The LNWR was well aware that problems could arise in periods of rough weather and, at such times, watchmen were placed to keep an eye on conditions around the tunnel area. On this furious night three platelayers were on duty at the west end of the tunnel. At around high tide, at about 10 p.m. the sea became very rough and washed over the track just as the up 'Irish Mail' was passing, sea water entering the carriages. Forty minutes later the last stopping train to Bangor passed through the tunnel and on to Penmaenmawr safely, followed half an hour later by an express goods from Manchester to Holyhead. It was this train which was to be caught up in the disaster.

At about 10.45 p.m. the watchmen noticed that the rails were completely covered by sea water, caused by a breach in the sea wall, though it was some 20 feet high and 6 feet thick at the base. The clatter of falling masonry was lost upon the watchmen through the roaring of the sea, which had washed away the ballast and ground underneath to leave the rails suspended over a gaping hole. The train was due; one of the watchmen immediately entered the tunnel with a warning lamp but this was too late to prevent the accident. At the inquest the watchman said that owing to a curve in the tunnel, the train was upon him before he realised it. He waved his lamp and shouted for it to stop but the noise of the storm made it difficult for him to be heard. The engine, however, whistled as it went past and the watchmen assumed that the driver had noticed something.

The driver almost certainly did see the warning light for he was applying his brakes and the reversing lever was set in reverse when he approached the damaged section of the track.

This became apparent at the inquest, from the testimony of the guard; he had noticed that the engine was slowing rapidly as it came out of the tunnel and accordingly applied the brakes in the brake van at the rear.

When the locomotive was recovered it was found to be set in reverse.....

The train, an LNWR 0-6-0 Ramsbottom 'DX' tender engine with twelve wagons and a brake van went over the damaged track which immediately collapsed, sending the locomotive with driver, fireman and eight wagons into the pit created by the sea, completely submerging them. Both the driver and the fireman were killed, presumed drowned.

The guard, and a passenger in the brake van, were unaware that the front portion of the train had been involved in the accident. The guard thought the train had broken in half and instructed his passenger to warn Penmaenmawr.

When the tide subsided the following morning, the engine was found on its side with a length of rail twisted underneath it. The tender had come down on top of it, with the debris of the wagons and their cargoes smashed in a heap and scattered around the immediate area. The body of the driver was washed up four miles or so away, on Conwy Morfa on the following morning but the fireman was never found.

The inquest felt that there was no need for a Board of Trade Enquiry as the disaster was due to the natural action of the sea and not any mechanical or structural defect. The verdict on the driver, after confusion between the Coroner and the jury, was accidental death.

The wreckage was removed the week after the accident; a by-pass line had been installed and a new, much stronger, wall was under construction, although train services were restored some 30 hours after the accident occurred. This new wall has never been breached by the sea since that fateful night.

The morning after the storms which caused the disaster on 12th January 1899. The engine and its train became visible as the sea water subsided.

Courtesy Penmaenmawr Historical Society)

29

The damage done to the sea wall and the railway track can be seen here. When the sea wall was rebuilt a stone commemorating the incident was inserted at the spot where the disaster occurred. In the background is Penmaenbach tunnel.
(Courtesy Penmaenmawr Historical Society)

Rescue workers and onlookers at the scene of the disaster, after the tide had ebbed.
(Courtesy Penmaenmawr Historical Society)

The disaster could have been far worse had the sea washed away the ballast some three quarters of an hour earlier, or two hours later, in both cases a speeding 'Irish Mail' was passing and loss of life would certainly have been greater. The latter train was halted at Penmaenmawr and passengers, with their luggage, were transferred by road to Conwy to join another train. In this case there was both disaster and a near miss.

Penmaenbach tunnel was again the scene of an incident 18 years later which could have been worse but for the prompt action of four employees of the railway company.... At midnight on Saturday January 26th 1917, four platelayers were working in the tunnel; just after the London bound 'Irish Mail' passed by they heard a noise and found to some considerable consternation that part of the tunnel *was beginning to cave in.*

Two of these platelayers, Morris Williams and William Williams, ran in opposite directions from the growing heap of debris which had fallen from the roof. Morris Williams climbed over the pile and ran through the tunnel towards Conwy, waving his lamp as an express for Holyhead, carrying troops on war leave from France, was approaching. The driver saw the light in time to apply the brakes and stopped the train a short distance from the fall.

William Williams who was running towards Penmaenmawr station, fell a number of times badly injuring himself but he managed to stop a goods train by shouting and waving his lamp. Morris Williams was considered a hero by the troops on the train when they realised what had happened and three days after the event all four platelayers were summoned to Crewe to be thanked by the Directors of the London and North Western

Mr. Morris Williams, one of the four platelayers who prevented a major catastrophe in 1917. It was Mr. Williams who managed to stop the express to Holyhead; running through the tunnel he was proclaimed a hero by the passengers on board.

(Courtesy Mrs. E.A. Hitches)

Railway Company. Later the same day at the entrance to Penmaenbach tunnel, Morris Williams was presented with an award of £5 and the other three were given £3 each. When Morris Williams retired in 1936, he was presented with a gold watch by his workmates in recognition of his courage on that night in 1917.

The subsequent investigation into the rockfall inside the tunnel revealed the cause to be a small waterfall, which had frozen and stretched the supporting girders beyond breaking point, bringing down 150 tons of rock and earth on to the rails.

There is little doubt that the prompt action of these four platelayers prevented a major accident and great loss of life. The express to Holyhead was packed and had it hit the rockfall then many would have died and there would have been great difficulties in reaching the injured. The goods train travelling in the opposite direction would have inflicted even greater loss of life.

The only accident to occur within the immediate vicinity of Penmaenmawr station took place at 3.05 a.m. on 27th August 1950, when the up 'Irish Mail' hit a light engine, causing six deaths and thirty seven injuries.

At 2.52 a.m. a solitary engine, class 5MT 2-6-0 'Crab' No. 42885, arrived tender first at the down platform from Llandudno Junction, to collect a train of stone wagons from the sidings. The engine pulled up at the signalbox before crossing on to the up line in order to enter the sidings to couple up its train and then take it to Mold Junction. The up 'Irish Mail' running some 30 minutes late, had been accepted by the signalman at 2.50 a.m. just before the light engine had arrived.

42885 crossed over on to the up line, whistled and waited for the poir ts to be changed so that it could enter the sidings. At this moment some confusion arose and the light engine did not

set back into the sidings as expected and crossed the points set clear for the up line. At the same time, the signals were set to 'clear' to allow the 'Irish Mail' to pass through. The driver apparently misunderstood the signal and thought that he should go back to Llandudno Junction as a light engine and started to move slowly forward, then he stopped and waited for his firemen to join him on the footplate. The fireman was walking back from the sidings, wondering what was happening when he heard the sound of the 'Irish Mail' coming from the west. He waved his red lamp as a warning to the signalman that the light engine was still on the up main line, and the signalman immediately set the signals back to danger. Once the driver of the 'Crab' realised what was happening, he started to move forward, in an attempt to get clear of the express train which was following.

The 'Irish Mail' was travelling at around 70 mph in order to make up time (5 mph within the speed limit) when the driver saw the signal change from green to red; he immediately applied the brakes but was unable to prevent the train hitting the light engine just beyond the crossover into the sidings at the east end of the station.

The 'Irish Mail' was travelling at around 70 mph in order to make up time (5 mph within the speed limit) when the driver saw the signal light changed from green to red; he immediately applied the brakes but was unable to prevent the train hitting the light engine just beyond the crossover into the sidings at the east of the station.

Lancashire Fusilier smote nearly halfway into the tender of the light engine, derailing two rear wheels. All wheels of the 'Royal Scot' were derailed, the front bogie became detached and was thrown to one side but because the engine was locked into the tender of the 'Crab' it kept a straight course as it propelled it some 240 yards forward, tearing up the track as it went.

The express engine became uncoupled from the train, the brake vehicle immediately behind it pitching violently as it ran into the damaged track, rising into the air and plunging downwards into the ballast. As the underframe rose, the underframe of the 1st class sleeping car was driven below it and the sleeping car telescoped into the brake, totally destroying it and killing five of its occupants.

The telescoping of the first two vehicles absorbed much of the shock and the third and fourth coaches remained upright, the fifth and sixth coaches were thrown on their right hand sides and slewed across both running lines, parallel to each other, the seventh coach was also on its right hand side, about 45 degrees to the track alignment with the leading end crushed as it and the sixth coach folded together. The eighth, ninth and tenth coaches were derailed but remained upright. The last six coaches remained upright on the track as they came to a stop.

At the time of the crash a heavy goods train was due from Llandudno Junction and the signalman immediately set the signals to danger on the down line. The driver of the express, although injured, as was the fireman, also realised that the goods train was due, and he told the fireman to place detonators to warn the oncoming train. The goods driver saw the signals turn from green to red and almost at once he heard the detonators and braked hard, stopping about 100 yards before he would have hit the two coaches lying across the down line. The fireman of the express was found unconscious a little later by the side of the down line with a box of detonators at his side, the goods engine received slight damage as it brushed past the derailed express engine. It was as well that the goods train was stopped as it contained ammunition and had the collision occurred with the coaches lying across the track then there may well have been a devastating explosion and great loss of life.

A general view of the wreckage caused when the 'Irish Mail' collided with a light engine in the early hours of the 27th August 1950. Most fatalities occurred in the wooden sleeping car, which was totally wrecked, as can be seen in the foreground.
(Courtesy Gwynedd Archives

Immediately after the crash the signalman woke up the station master who went out to help while his wife telephoned for medical assistance. Many local people came to the station with blankets and sheets in order to help. The cafe opposite to the station was opened within a few minutes and dispensed free tea and coffee to the uninjured. Reg Lunt, a local St. John Ambulance man, arrived at the scene at around 4 a.m. and describes 'a shambles with trains piled into each other'. He stayed on, administering emergency first aid, until 8 a.m. on the following Monday morning.

The station itself was used as a casualty clearing house until ambulances arrived and ferried the injured to local hospitals. Repair gangs from Chester and Crewe worked through the whole of Sunday to Monday morning when single working on the down track was restored by 12.51 a.m. Normal working was achieved by 8.15 a.m. an interruption of 29¼ hours.

The Ministry of Transport report on the accident concluded that the view from the signalbox to the junction of the sidings at the east end of the station was obscured by the footbridge and hand signals could not easily been seen. This was important when movements on to sidings were controlled by hand signals or lamp signals, as was the case at Penmaenmawr. Obstruction of the view from the signal box could lead to misunderstandings and this was most certainly the case in this instance. Had British Railways not been planning to make changes to signalling at this time, then the Inquiry would almost certainly have insisted that a new signal box be put up at the eastern end of the station, opposite the sidings. The busy nature of the traffic led the Inquiry to consider the use of track circuiting and ground signals and these were duly recommended.

The opening of the new signal box in 1953 was almost certainly expedited as a result of this accident, the worst, with the greatest loss of life and number of injuries ever experienced at Penmaenmawr. Only quick thinking on the part of the signalman and engine crew prevented great loss of life.

Accidents and near misses around Penmaenmawr have been mercifully few in the 140 years since the station opened, an extraordinarily good record when the quantity of traffic passing through is taken into account.

The accident of 1950 produced the highest number of casualties of any railway incident around Penmaenmawr. The damage to the two locomotives can clearly be seen after they have been separated by railway engineers.

J. Smith

WORLD WAR TWO;
THE CENTENARY

The outbreak of the Second World War brought the railways under Government control, as they had been during the Great War some 25 years earlier. That war would come was apparent by 1937 and preparations for the takeover of the railways were made by 1938. A real fear was attack from the air, an increasing possibility after experiences in the Spanish Civil War when German aircraft bombed open towns. Evacuation schemes were prepared in Britain around the same period. The railways were taken over by the Government when war became absolutely inevitable, on 1st September 1939, and during the first four days of September the mass evacuation of civilians, mostly children, from the major cities was undertaken without problem. Some of these children came to Penmaenmawr to be billeted on the local community, and a few stayed for the duration, forging friendships which would last a lifetime. Along with the children, Government Departments were established in the town, away from the centres of enemy action and were situated in the Grand Hotel. The staff of these departments came to the town by train.

Wartime measures introduced by the Government included the drastic reduction of passenger trains and speeds were limited to 60 mph to reduce maintenance requirements. These reductions were more drastic than those imposed during the First World War. The 'phoney war' allowed some of these restrictions to be relaxed and speed limits were raised to 75 mph for express trains in December 1939. By Whitsun 1940, the railways were planning extra trains for holidaymakers but the German invasion of the Low Countries put a stop to this, for trains would be needed to bring soldiers away from the southern ports of England, consequent upon the retreat from Dunkirk. From this point on, passenger trains were severely restricted and the population was discouraged from travelling, the railways displaying posters asking *IS YOUR JOURNEY REALLY NECESSARY?* Although travel was difficult often with substantial delays and overcrowded trains, many people did make train journeys and the holiday trade in Penmaenmawr continued to thrive as the war weary came from cities like Liverpool and Manchester, which had suffered badly from the blitz.

Penmaenmawr was spared the bombing of mainland Britain, the blitz and its aftermath and railway traffic was not disrupted in the immediate area; thus the town was a very safe place in which to reside. The only enemy aircraft in the area were overflying in order to attack Liverpool. In fact the only damage experienced locally occurred near Conwy, when a German aircraft jettisoned its bombs in an effort to escape ground fire.

The quarries were busy during the war years as the stone was very good for the manufacture of concrete. It had been so used in the 1930s, in bank strongrooms and in the construction of the Mersey Tunnel. In the years preceding World War Two concrete from Penmaenmawr stone found its way into many Government contracts, including a factory at Chorley, Lancashire. During the war it went to make aerodrome runways, roads and shelters and, along with railway ballast, required to repair bomb damaged track, enormous tonnages of stone left the town, on an increasingly overstretched railway system.

When peace did return in 1945 the railway was in a dilapidated condition, needing substantial labour and funding to bring it back to pre-war standards. The LMS estimated that it would cost £14 million, at 1945 prices, to catch up with arrears of track and signal maintenance, and a further £26 million to bring its track up to pre-war standards.

The other railway companies had problems too. The Depression before the war and competition from road transport had left the company short of money and in the years prior to 1939 the shareholders had received no dividend on their investments. Furthermore the Government had made a promise that the railways would receive similar revenue to that yielded in a successful peacetime year. That this did not happen was due to the Government backing down on this promise and the railways ended up treated in even worse fashion than after World War One. Under a retrospective Agreement backdated to 1st December 1940, the railways obtained less than half the revenue they had earned from wartime traffic, the balance being taken by the Treasury. The railways were also inadequately compensated for damage by enemy action and so bore much of the reconstruction costs themselves. All of this left them with inadequate funds to reinstate the system to the levels which would have existed had there been no war.

Post war reconstruction nevertheless brought benefits to the railway in Penmaenmawr. Stone was required for concrete, tar coated stone for the roads and railway ballast was still in demand. The LMS recognised this in their 1947 publication tracing the route of the 'Irish Mail' in which the Co. noted that passengers owed much of their comfort and smooth travelling to good ballast from the granite face of this mountain headland.

Change in attitude of the population of Britain following the wartime feeling of 'all pulling together for the war effort' brought a landslide victory for the Labour party in the General Election of 1945. The new Government was established on a policy of the Welfare State and Nationalisation of major industries which included the railways. The companies tried to resist this takeover but the rank and file welcomed the change and their efforts were of no avail.

The 1947 *Transport Act* envisaged a nationalised integrated transport system with the railways the main carriers and buses and lorries acting as feeders. The Government had recognised the growing importance of roads and, rather than have it competing with the railways, felt that it would be better to have the two forms working together. The Act took effect from 1st January 1948, the new undertaking to be divided into six different regions known as British Railways. At nationalisation Penmaenmawr ceased to be part of the old London Midland and Scottish Railway and became a station on the London Midland Region of British Railways, with high hopes for the future.

Penmaenmawr was still a very busy place at its centenary in 1949. Passenger traffic was still substantial, with many holidaymakers passing through. The quarry sidings were well developed and stone traffic was being moved in ever increasing quantities. The original station siding, with the goods shed, was still in place and goods were delivered to it frequently, not least domestic coal for the local coal merchant.

The previous hundred years had seen the station grow from a small halt to an important stop for passengers and freight on the main line from London to Holyhead, the sidings on the up line had been expanded enormously from their inception and its economic importance to the town was clearly recognised.

The second hundred years started with optimism but changes were on the way which would lead to the run down of passenger traffic and the threat of closure.

The western end of Penmaenmawr station, looking west in 1964. The original signalbox is just below the footbridge, built in 1884. Following an accident with a BR crane in February 1990, the bridge is now supported by railway sleepers. The slate roofed station canopy is supported by cast iron columns, as was the old waiting shelter.

(Lens of Sutton)

THE 'FIFTIES

The 1950s dawned with increasing competition for the railways. The post-war consumer boom continued, bringing increasing prosperity and full employment; this created an ever increasing demand for motor cars, threatening all forms of public transport, but the greatest effect was felt by the railways, particularly at the many stations not in the centres of the towns they served.

Despite this, rail traffic through Penmaenmawr remained heavy and brought its fair share of passengers. There was even a substantial increase during the Suez crisis of 1957, when severe petrol rationing brought the public back to the railways. During Suez passenger traffic reached a new post-war peak. Fare increases and the inflated passenger figures however only served to mask the real effects of road competition; the truth was that the railways were losing money at an alarming rate.

They were also facing a severe threat to freight traffic from lorries. In the early 1950s the railways were still 'Common Carriers', forced to accept anything presented for despatch, to anywhere in the Kingdom at a fixed rate set by legislation. Road transport firms were not affected by these restrictions and could accept or refuse loads if they wished, and could fix their own charges, thereby undercutting the railway. In order to equalise competition between road and railway the Conservative Government which had been elected in 1950 denationalised road transport and brought in the 1953 *Transport Act*, which abolished the 'Common Carrier' liabilities and allowed freedom to select traffic and charge an economic price for services. While this was a move in the right direction, it came too late to prevent the loss of much freight traffic to road.

The quarries in Penmaenmawr were making increasing use of lorries and in 1955 a hopper was built in Bell Yard on the quarry site to load them. A tar coating plant was built adjacent to this hopper in the same year and all of this production was lost to the railway. The only material leaving the sidings in any large quantity by this time was track ballast. A reflection of this was that the Brundritt (Wrights) sidings were closed and all track lifted in 1952. The jetty closed at the same time and was demolished in 1959.

The post war years of full employment and improved industrial conditions, creating cleaner and healthier working environments, made for problems of staff recruitment on the railway; the work offered grim conditions, in steam engine sheds and elsewhere, and difficult hours. Staffing levels and the quality of coal fell leaving BR increasingly insolvent.

To try to alleviate these problems, the Government authorised the *Modernization Plan* in 1955. An expenditure of £1,240 million was envisaged, the bulk of it to be spent on new traction and rolling stock. The original plan was for large scale electrification, with diesels introduced as a short term measure to replace steam 'as soon as possible'.

The implementation of the *Modernization Plan* brought some benefit to the quarries and the sidings at Penmaenmawr. Diesel locomotives were heavier than the steam engines they replaced; it meant a thicker foundation of railway ballast and production was increased until it reached a maximum of 180,000 tons in 1960. All this extra ballast was despatched from the quarries by rail.

The station and its sidings assumed a new and novel role in 1954, when it was first used as an overnight stopping point for the Royal Train on the occasion of the Queen's visit to North Wales. The sidings have been so used on two further occasions; in 1963 and again in 1980, when the Prince of Wales came to the district. This last visit created some amusement in the town when one of the well known local railway enthusiasts decided to take photographs. Immediately finding himself arrested by the security guards this particular threat to the Royal person was only released when members of the local community persuaded the authorities that his presence was of a purely innocent nature. Our enthusiast was subsequently fined for trespassing on railway property. Many of the local people felt that he was treated somewhat harshly.

In 1960 the Minister of Transport, Ernest Marples, appointed a group of industrialists to recommend a role for the railways of the future. One member of this group was to have a profound effect on the future of Britains railway system, including Penmaenmawr station. His name was Dr. Richard Beeching.

A view of the station looking west, the main building on the left, and the old stone waiting shelter on the right. This was demolished in 1970 and replaced by a 'bus shelter' type structure.

(Lens of Sutton)

Special CHEAP DAY Tickets

Every day by any train

SUNDAYS WHERE SERVICE PERMITS

6th APRIL 1964
UNTIL FURTHER NOTICE
FROM

LLANFAIRFECHAN
LLANRWST & TREFRIW
PENMAENMAWR
PONT-Y-PANT
ROMAN BRIDGE
TAL-Y-CAFN & EGLWYSBACH

BETWS-Y-COED
BLAENAU FFESTINIOG
CONWAY
DOLGARROG
DOLWYDDELEN
GLAN CONWAY

RETURN ON DAY OF ISSUE ONLY

PASSENGERS MAY TERMINATE THE OUTWARD JOURNEY AT ANY INTERMEDIATE STATION ON SURRENDER OF THE OUTWARD HALF OF THEIR TICKET AND MAY RETURN FROM ANY INTERMEDIATE STATION.

Children under three years of age travel free; three and under fourteen years, half-fare.
(Fractions of ½d reckoned as ½d) The fares shown herein are subject to alteration.

TICKETS CAN BE OBTAINED IN ADVANCE FROM STATIONS

THIS PAMPHLET CANCELS FARES CONTAINED No. K.465.

Further information will be supplied on application to Station Official, Railway Agents, or to the ARUNDALE Divisional Manager, Chester — Tel: phone Chester 21900 (Ext. 231)

K.585

British Railways
LONDON MIDLAND REGION

Rebuilt Royal Scot No. 46156 The South Wales Borderer *leaves Penmaenmawr station in the early evening of 30th June 1962, with a semi-fast train to Holyhead.*

(Keith Smith)

SUMMERTIME BLUES

Holiday traffic in the 1950s and 1980s

The years from 1950 to 1960 were probably the last of intensive tourist rail traffic before the private car dealt such decisive and fatal blows to these services in the 1960s, 1970s and 1980s. The trains passing through or stopping at Penmaenmawr during the 1950s would, with some minor exceptions, have been similar to the type of service available during the 1930s, when the railway was still the principal way to a holiday.

The latter part of the 1950s probably saw railways in Britain more or less at a peak; a large measure of wartime recovery had been achieved and the road threat, though desperately close, was still relatively masked. In 1957 the 'Irish Mail' services at 8.45 p.m. from Euston and the 1.10 a.m. from Holyhead ran throughout the year and there were extra 'Irish Mail' trains at 8.15 a.m. from Euston, 1.25 p.m. (except Saturdays) and 4 p.m. (Saturdays only) from Holyhead at the height of the holiday season, from July 1st to the end of summer services, around mid-September. During the winter there were through services to and from Crewe, Liverpool, Manchester, Derby, Birmingham and London (Euston) and on summer Saturdays trains to Bradford, Burton-upon-Trent, Cheadle, Leamington Spa, Leeds, Leicester, Morley, Northampton, Newcastle-upon-Tyne, Nottingham, Rugby, Sheffield, Smethwick, Stechford, Stafford, Etruria, Leek, Leigh (Staffs), Stoke-on-Trent, Walsall and such places as Accrington, Bacup, Blackburn, Blyth Bridge, Bolton, Burnley, Ford Green, Colne, Clayton West, Glasgow, Hadfield, Huddersfield, Oldham, Preston, Rochdale, Stockton, Swinton Town and Tyldesley.

Passenger trains through Penmaenmawr could be divided into four groups; the 'Irish Mail', trains to and from Butlins holiday camp at Penychain, near Pwllheli, those serving resorts west of Llandudno Junction, and purely locals....

There were three down trains in 1957, to connect with the afternoon sailing from Holyhead to Ireland, the 10 a.m. from Manchester (Exchange) and the 8.05 a.m. and 8.15 a.m. from Euston. All of these ran non-stop from Chester to Holyhead. There was, also, a 9.20 a.m. Crewe to Holyhead which called at all principal stations, designed to connect with this boat. The up trains meeting with the afternoon sailings from Ireland to Holyhead were the 3.30 p.m. and 4.00 p.m. Holyhead to Euston, the 4.10 p.m. to Birmingham and the 4.20 p.m. to Manchester.

A night boat left Holyhead at 3.25 a.m. and principal trains connecting with it were the 5.35 p.m., 8.45 p.m. and 8.52 p.m. from Euston, the 10.10 p.m. and 10.20 p.m. from Manchester and the 10.00 p.m. from Birmingham, which only ran on Fridays. There was an additional boat from Holyhead at 6.30 a.m. on Saturdays and connecting trains including the 12.25 a.m. from Manchester and the 11.45 p.m. from Euston.

Passengers on the night boat from Ireland left Holyhead at 1.10 a.m. and 1.35 a.m. for Euston, 1.25 a.m. for Birmingham and 1.50 a.m. for Manchester. There were additional sailings on Friday and Saturday nights and trains left Holyhead at 11.00 p.m., 11.15 .m. and 11.30 p.m. The 11.00 p.m. on Friday nights went to Paddington. If demand required, there were relief trains leaving Holyhead at 3.45 a.m., 4.00 a.m. and 4.15 a.m.

The traffic through to Butlin's holiday camp was quite substantial and included the 8.05 a.m. and 8.15 a.m. from

Manchester (Exchange), the 10.15 a.m. from Warrington and the 9.35 a.m. from Liverpool (Lime Street). The 10.15 a.m. from Warrington started from a different place each Saturday usually one of the Lancashire towns on holiday that week. On August Bank Holiday the train originated from Stoke-on-Trent.

Trains leaving Butlins at Penychain included the 8.45 a.m. to Stoke-on-Trent, the 9.40 a.m. to Manchester, the 10.05 a.m. to Liverpool, the 11.25 a.m. to Warrington, which was usually extended as required, and the 12.05 p.m. to Manchester.

Other trains passing through Penmaenmawr included the 6.37 a.m. Afonwen to Manchester, the 3.02 p.m. Llandudno Junction to Holyhead, the 2.15 p.m. Caernarfon to Liverpool, the 11.15 'Welshman' from Euston to Bangor, the 5.48 local from Bangor to Llandudno Junction, the 4.25 p.m. Crewe to Bangor. As well as this traffic there were also locals which would stop at least every hour at Penmaenmawr.

'Black 5' 4-6-0 No. 44907 about to depart from Penmaenmawr with a train for Bangor during 1953. The old LNWR signalbox has been replaced by the more modern structure at the eastern end of the platform, a result of the accident of 1950.

(Gwyn Roberts)

Ex-LMS unrebuilt Royal Scot No. 46163 Civil Service Rifleman *stands in front of the second Penmaenmawr signalbox (then situated at the west end of the station on the down line) as it waits to depart with a train for Bangor, during the summer of 1951.*

(*Gwyn Roberts*)

BR Britannia Pacific No. 70048 with the up 'Irish Mail', passes the now-defunct Brundrit sidings just west of the railway station in 1954, shortly after entering service with British Railways.

(*Gwyn Roberts*)

Apart from passenger trains there were also numerous goods, both through freight and stone traffic from the quarry sidings. On Saturdays in the summertime there was very little; after the 6.40 a.m. Mold Junction to Menai Bridge, there was no further working until 5.35 p.m. the Holyhead to Mold Junction and the 5.55 p.m. Mold Junction to Menai Bridge. One other non-passenger train was the 12.15 p.m. van train from Holyhead to Manchester which frequently stopped en route to attach or detach vans as required.

During the week there were other 'special' holiday trains including the 'scenic excursion' to Llanfair P.G. on Sundays and the 'Land Cruises' which ran four times a day between Llandudno, Rhyl, Corwen, Barmouth, Caernarfon and Llandudno, passing through Penmaenmawr.

Some thirty years later the summer timetable for 1987 looks very different. Gone are the trains to Butlins and to Caernarfon, as well as to Llanberis, since those branches were closed in the 1960s as part of the Beeching rationalisation. Visitors to Butlins holiday camp now mostly travel by car or motor coach.

The 'Land Cruises' have long since gone, replaced by motor coach trips run by operators from Llandudno even though this probably means sitting in traffic jams for some while, as the roads are now choked with so many vehicles and coaches that they can no longer cope in high summer.

The 'Irish Mail' service has been depleted since the 1950s; the first leaves Crewe at 12.15 a.m. (except Mondays), followed by the 9.35 a.m., the 10.00 p.m. on weekdays and 9.50 p.m. on Saturdays from Euston. Workings from Holyhead are the 1.15 a.m. and the 12.55 p.m. with none on Sundays. Others to Holyhead include the 'Holidaymakers Express' leaving Birmingham at 8.23 a.m. on Saturdays only, the 'Welsh Dragon' from Euston at 4.15 p.m. on weekdays only, and 'The Welshman' from Cardiff at 5.35 p.m.

Local trains serving Penmaenmawr run every two hours from 7.44 a.m. to 9.11 p.m. from Llandudno Junction and from 7.25 a.m. to 9.03 p.m. from Bangor during the week and on Saturdays. Services on Sunday are at 12.36 p.m. 1.59 p.m, 5.22 p.m. and 7.48 p.m. from Llandudno Junction and 10.14 a.m., 3.08 p.m., 5.09 p.m., 6.14 p.m. and 6.50 p.m. from Bangor. The passenger service in Penmaenmawr was strengthened in 1988 to an hourly service in recognition of the competition posed by the new express way.

Freight through Penmaenmawr includes the occasional train of nuclear waste from Wylfa Power Station, at least one ballast train leaving Penmaenmawr sidings every week day and a train, usually double headed by a pair of class 37 diesel locomotives, carrying roadstone for Hope Street Manchester, every Friday. There is also a small number of freights passing through in the week; unlike the 1950s there is no freight traffic at all during weekends.

Excursion trains west of Llandudno Junction are non-existent and relief trains are rare, no more than two on a Saturday. The reduction in traffic over the last thirty years is almost certainly due to the rapid increase in private car ownership since the 1950s as well as increased motor coach traffic which, in most cases, is cheaper than the railway.

Stone traffic has disappeared during the weekends as most production ceases on Fridays and does not re-commence until Monday; this usually means that there would be no staff at destinations to receive deliveries. Weekday freight traffic has been much reduced because of competition from lorries which can deliver door to door and undercut the railway on price. Although using lorries is not necessarily more efficient the road lobby has been so powerful in recent years that freight which should have gone by rail, including much container traffic from Holyhead, has been taken by juggernaut lorries, blocking the narrow roads along the North Wales coast.

Approaching Penmaenmawr station from the west is Ivatt 2-6-2 tank No. 41234 with a stopping train for Llandudno Junction, during the summer of 1955

(Gwyn Roberts)

Fairburn 2-6-4 tank No. 42261, then only two years old, leaves Penmaenmawr with a local for Llandudno Junction in l951.

(Gwyn Roberts)

Ex-LMS Jubilee 4-6-0 No. 45686 St. Vincent *passes beneath the bridge just west of the station, which carried the narrow gauge railway into the sidings. The structure above contains belts, which carried stone to hoppers for loading wagons in those same sidings.*

(Gwyn Roberts)

A parcels train nears the overbridge to the Youth Hostel at Penmaenbach, east of Penmaenmawr station, heading towards Conway on a summers day in the 1960s.

(Peter Owen)

DECLINE

Two factors combined to effect the decline of the tourist trade in Penmaenmawr and, in consequence, greatly reduce traffic through the station. The first was the change in the type of holidays which people were taking - no longer were they coming to the town in large numbers, drawn away by the new 'package holiday', to Spain in particular where sunshine was guaranteed. While other towns on the North Wales coast, notably Rhyl and Llandudno, were well established as true holiday resorts and fared reasonably well when competition grew, Penmaenmawr did not invest sufficient money to develop its tourist potential and could not compete.

By the middle of the 1960s the numbers of people coming to holiday in Penmaenmawr began to fall substantially and while the town still had some visitors, the tourist trade largely collapsed. Penmaenmawr became a dormitory with its population working in other towns along the coast. Passenger usage of the station began to fall and, in conseqence, train services were reduced.

The second factor, and possibly the most important was the Beeching Report and the threat of closure, which may have convinced many potential visitors that the town was not worth visiting if it did not have a railway service. Dr. Richard Beeching became the first Chairman of the new British Railways Board which had been created by the 1962 Transport Act. The intention of this new legislation was to reduce the BR financial deficit through the adoption of a management approach to operations.

At the end of March 1963 Dr Beeching issued his 'Reshaping Report' in an effort to reduce the railways' deficits. The plan envisaged the closure of over 5,000 miles of track and 2,350 stations, arguing that they were hopelessly uneconomic.

The one major fault with his argument concerned the main trunk routes. Beeching argued that the retention of these alone would concentrate more traffic on to them, but closure rather than simplification of the branches created a 'domino effect' and drew further traffic to the roads. The loss of the branches caused the collapse of the economies of adjoining lines as they lost feeder business to the roads. This principle applied to Penmaenmawr as the the Caernarfon, Afonwen, Llanberis and Amlwch branches closed.

The 'Reshaping Report' advocated the closure of all stations on the North Wales Coast line except Rhyl, Colwyn Bay, Llandudno Junction, Llandudno, Bangor and Holyhead as well as the branches. The British Railways Board announced that these stations would close within the next eighteen months. Penmaenmawr was therefore scheduled for closure by the end of 1964. British Railways justified the plan, arguing that rail traffic was diminishing on the North Wales coast and it would be uneconomic for all stations and branches to remain open.

Like the rest of Great Britain, the Report was received with horror at Penmaenmawr. While some felt that closure of the station would make little difference to the tourist potential of the town, there was the recognition that without it holiday-makers would choose to go to a resort where a full railway service did exist.

Penmaenmawr Council wrote to the Minister of Transport pointing out the disastrous effect on the tourist trade if the station were to close and requested a coach service to run between Colwyn Bay, Llandudno Junction and Bangor, should it be forced upon the town. By May 1963 local Councils were asking to take over the running of threatened stations, for the feeling was that closure would severely affect tourism. Seeing the opportunity to profit from the monopoly to be gained by closure of local railway stations, the Crosville Bus Company applied to increase its fares and met with little opposition. This did, however, help to concentrate action

against closure and a Conference of Caernarfonshire County Councils declared itself 'appalled' by the economic conseqences.

Throughout the year there was much debate and discussion over the proposals. Whilst much of this centred upon the Blaenau Ffestiniog branch and the disastrous economic effects of its demise there was, equally, recognition of the potential damage to the tourist trade along the North Wales coast. The news for the railway in Penmaenmawr was not all bad however. Much of the stone from the quarries, formerly despatched by sea, was now going by rail; by 1963 two trains of crushed stone per week were being sent to Manchester, with two further loads of a similar quantity going to Liverpool, and there were still several trains of ballast leaving the sidings every week.

An incident which was to spell the beginning of the end of stone movement by sea occurred in November 1967 when the *Rethi Muller* called at the Darbishire jetty for a cargo. While she was berthed stormy weather caused a line to break and the ship was beached; it took two weeks to refloat her. Much of the problem was due to the size of the ship and it was realised that such vessels were too large to use the jetty on a regular basis. Following this incident the only ships to call did so on a casual basis in case a load was available. This arrangement persisted until 1976, the last ship calling in the summer of that year after which the jetty was closed. Most of the sea traffic afterwards went by road but the railway still managed to take many of the heavier consignments.

The pressure of the local Authorities paid off when closures were finally implemented in 1966. Conwy station closed that year, only to be reopened twenty one years later, and Penmaenmawr station was to have closed at the same time. Along with Llanfairfechan, and other stations on Anglesey, the axe did not fall as expected and Penmaenmawr was eventually reprieved in 1967. The extent of the sidings and the business emanating from them almost certainly saved the day, although the local councils have had to fight to keep the station open ever since.

Through passenger traffic was reduced, partly through rationalisation and partly because of closure of branches further west. The sidings serving the quarries continued to be quite busy and there was still a considerable quantity of freight traffic using Penmaenmawr.

The freighter Rethi Muller aground for two weeks in November 1967. This incident spelt the beginning of the end for removal of stone by sea at Penmaenmawr.

(Gwyn Roberts)

Class 24 No. 24082 passes Penmaenmawr station and the site of the old goods siding, with a train of empty freightliner wagon flats from Holyhead on the evening of 17th March 1978.

(*Ron Watson-Jones*)

CHANGE IN THE 1970s & 1980s

Following the demise of steam through Penmaenmawr at the end of March 1967, changes were taking place at the station which illustrated its diminishing importance. The large waiting shelter on the up platform was demolished in 1970 and replaced by a bus shelter type structure, still in use today. Part of the main building at the east end of the down platform was also demolished at this time and the gas lamps were disconnected and replaced by electric light.

The original signal box was demolished (as noted earlier) after use as a storeroom on its decommissioning and replacement by the LNWR box on the opposite platform. It seems a pity that this unique relic of the old Chester and Holyhead Railway could not have found its way into preservation. Perhaps it may well have done so had demolition taken place some years later.

The original siding at the west end of the station beyond the down platform had been used purely for coal deliveries to a local merchant in recent years and this traffic was eventually concentrated at Llandudno. The result was that the sidings and its goods shed closed on 4th May 1964 and in 1970 the track was lifted. The shed itself survived and was left derelict until a local road haulier took it over in 1981 for use as a lorry depot, ironically to move stone products from the quarry, some of which once went by rail. While the quarry sidings were still busy the cripple siding, a small length of track on the promenade side of the layout, was clipped out of use in the middle 1970s and finally lifted when the subway under the station from the road to the promenade was strengthened in 1982.

Winter storms have caused some damage to the signal box in recent years. The roof was blown off during gales in the mid-1970s and the windows were blown out in 1986. These were replaced by small ones, still in use today.

Traffic in the quarry sidings was mainly made up of railway ballast trains during the 1970s and 80s, with several leaving the town each week. In this period the last jetty for seaborne traffic was closed (1976 - see earlier) and finally demolished in 1983 when shipping of stone ceased. Some of the traffic generated by the loss of shipping went to the railway but almost all of it went by road. The remodelling of Crewe station in 1984 created an increased demand for ballast and traffic increased accordingly until the contract was finished.

Traffic along the A55 trunk road from Chester had become a serious problem by the end of the 1970s and plans were drawn up to construct an expressway to improve this route. The section near the station was planned to pass between the quarry sidings and the sea and in order to accommodate the road, a narrow and simpler sidings complex was installed in 1986, a new wagon loading hopper of 5000 tons having come into use on 10th October 1984. The new arrangement has only four tracks, with a facility just short of the hoppers to uncouple the locomotive and allow it to run light to the other end of its train. The wagons are then pushed below the hopper and the locomotive is used to bring the wagons forward as they are loaded.

Along with the remodelling of the sidings, a new signalling system was installed and the old semaphore signals, which had existed for over a century, both as lower quadrant LNWR and

A portrait of class 40 No. 40106 in the quarry sidings at Penmaenmawr station in September 1977, with a train of empty hoppers ready for loading with railway ballast.

Ron Watson-Jones

Three two car diesel multiple units making up an all stations train to Manchester passes under the footbridge connecting the beach with the housing estate, on the left of the picture, at the eastern end of Penmaenmawr in the mid-1970s. This footbridge was replaced by a more modern structure in 1987 as part of the A55 expressway development. Virtually all of the grassland in the foreground was washed away during the winter storms of 1990 and was replaced by a new sea defence of boulders and stone from the quarry.

(Gwyn Roberts)

upper quadrant BR types were replaced by three aspect colour light signals, only one of which is placed at the station (at the east end of the up platform).

In early 1988 the entrance to the granite sidings was remodelled using facing points on the up and down lines, allowing trains from the east to cross into the sidings without need to reverse. The new layout is approximately 100 yards east of the signalbox, just beyond the western portal of a new tunnel carrying the A55 expressway over the main line and on to the old promenade.

Before the remodelling stone trains entered the station and reversed on to the up line before entering the sidings at points situated directly opposite to the signal box. A three aspect signal has also been installed to protect this new junction.

As the tourist industry continued its decline during the 1970s and 1980s less and less passengers were using the station. While express trains continued to call right through to the last year or two, the number of passengers using them did not really justify the service. When the summer schedules were published for 1987 no expresses were listed to call at Penmaenmawr, the only long distance workings being the 'all stations' Sprinter trains to and from Hull. Even these have now ceased, having been cut back to terminate at Manchester.

The reopening of Conwy station during the summer of 1987 brought extra interest when a shuttle service between Llandudno Junction and Conwy was introduced. The only point where it could cross over to return to Llandudno Junction was at Penmaenmawr and the train came into the station empty from Conwy in order to reverse and return there empty. This practice was discontinued when the sidings entrance was remodelled.

At 11.45 a.m. on 30th January 1980 class 40 No. 40007 waits to enter the sidings to collect a ballast train whilst 40030 Scythia departs from the station with the 11.30 am Bangor-Manchester train.

(Ron Watson-Jones)

THE STATION TODAY

The end of the 1987 summer timetable brought a reduction of status to Penmaenmawr, when the station became an unmanned halt. The Local Authority had objected to the proposal when it was first suggested, arguing that there was risk to life of people, mainly children, on the station particularly with the amount of stone traffic still using the sidings, and it was felt that a member of staff would prevent any risk of this. British Rail, however, did not relent and, along with Llanfairfechan, there ceased to be staff at Penmaenmawr from 5th October 1987.

This loss has meant that the station is a very quiet place, with an almost ghostly quality. This is most apparent at weekends when there are no stone trains, and less workings on the main line. All door signs have been removed, leaving patchy paintwork and giving an impression of tattiness and neglect. The fact that the signalbox is still in use and the sidings still have traffic, keeps a sort of railway 'staff presence' and has probably prevented the kind of vandalism and graffiti which usually occurs when a station building goes out of use.

A sense of the decline is reflected in the construction of the expressway on the old promenade next to the sidings. This is tangible evidence of the influence of road transport and its replacement of the railway as the main means of mass travel. For several years motorists have passed through the town to reach destinations which have become popular for tourism, as Penmaenmawr itself once was. The expressway opened in 1989, four months early, and allows passage through the area even more quickly than has been possible in the past. There is now no need to pass through the town centre and Penmaenmawr will presumably see less visitors than ever in summer. The loss of the promenade, until the new one was completed in the summer of 1989 has already had this effect with some visitors; seeing the mess created by the construction work, they have declared an unwillingness to return.

While there are trains stopping in the station at approximately hourly intervals, there are still the 'Irish Mails' and other expresses passing through, along with freight traffic to and from Anglesey, including spent nuclear fuel trains from Wylfa and container traffic from Holyhead.

The sidings serving the quarries are still busy with stone trains, mostly railway ballast traffic for British Rail. There is, also, a roadstone contract train which operates every Friday afternoon. This is made up of approximately 21 wagons, each carrying 64 tons of roadstone destined for Manchester. All of this traffic keeps a member of the railway staff, who used to be employed on the station, involved in the sidings.

Unusually, since the station has become an unmanned halt, there has been an improvement in the train service to and from the town. According to the winter timetable for 1987/88 there are to be three passenger trains to Llandudno Junction and three to Bangor on Sundays, something which had not occurred during the winter months for a few years past.

The exterior of the station showing its battered condition by 1987. The entrance is on the left through the gates.

(Gwyn Roberts)

'Problem' or 'Lady of the Lake' class 2-2-2 No 60 Tantalus. *An example of the successful locomotive type used on 'Irish Mail' services, running non-stop from Chester to Holyhead during the 1870s.*

(*Roger Carpenter Collection*)

An unidentified Webb 3-cylinder 2-2-2-0 compound of the 'Dreadnought' class waits at Penmaenmawr station with a train for Chester c.1898.

(*Roger Carpenter Collection*)

LOCOMOTIVES IN AND AROUND PENMAENMAWR

Situated on the route of the 'Irish Mail' Penmaenmawr has seen many of the 'top link' express locomotives of the old London and North Western Railway and in turn those of the London, Midland and Scottish Railway, and the nationalised British Railways. There were local trains powered by tank engines and later, diesel multiple units. The sidings saw many generations of powerful freight engines.

The first engines at Penmaenmawr were probably Trevithick 6ft. 2-2-2 singles or 5ft. 2-4-0 goods engines of the 'Crewe' type. These were nearly all given appropriate Welsh names to coincide with the opening of the line to Bangor. There was even one named *Penmaenmawr* (No. 295), introduced in 1852. Five years later this engine was transferred to the Lancaster and Carlisle Railway. The 6ft. 2-2-2 singles rarely carried names, but in 1852, after 100 of this type had been built, two did acquire names, Nos. 280 *Glendower* and 291 *Prince of Wales*.

After complaints about insufficient motive power in September 1850 and problems with some of the locomotives supplied by the LNWR notably 7ft. 2-2-2 No. 187 *Velocipede* and Crampton rear drive 7ft. 2-2-2 No 176 *Courier*, replacements were sent in the form of No. 290 *Rocket*, a 7ft 2-2-2 built at Crewe in 1852 and a new *Velocipede*, both based at Chester, No. 18 *Cerberus* built in July 1857 and the new *Pegasus* based at Holyhead. All four were to be used on the 'Irish Mail' and would have passed regularly through Penmaenmawr.

The four earlier engines were replaced in 1860 by new 7ft 6ins singles designed by Ramsbottom, known as the 'Problem' or 'Lady of the Lake' class, which ran the 'Irish Mail' until the 1880s. These trains were then running non-stop from Chester to Holyhead, running through Penmaenmawr at speed.

Another type of locomotive used on the Chester to Holyhead Railway was a further Ramsbottom design, a 6ft 7½in 2-4-0 'Newton' class engine which first appeared in 1866. Although primarily designed for use on Crewe to Carlisle expresses, they very soon found their way on to the Holyhead services and several were based at Chester and Llandudno. Many of these engines were later rebuilt by Francis Webb and were the pattern for the later 2-4-0 'Precedent' class. So successful were these engines that over a hundred were built.

Many of the Webb-designed engines appeared on the express trains passing through Penmaenmawr throughout the latter years of the nineteenth century and into the early years of the twentieth. These included 'Precedents', commonly known as 'Jumbos', the 4-4-0 four-cylinder compound 'Benbow' class, 'John Hick' 2-2-2-2 compounds and the four-cylinder compound 4-6-0s, commonly known as 'Bill Baileys'.

Local stopping trains and some pick-up goods trains were usually hauled by Webb 0-6-2 coal tank engines or 2-4-2 tanks. Many of these small engines survived in the area well into the twentieth century and could be seen hauling locals into the 1940s. The very heavy nature of the loads moved from the quarry sidings meant that shunting tanks were never used in Penmaenmawr, the work usually done by the train engines themselves. In the nineteenth century these engines were the Ramsbottom DX and Webb 'Coal' 0-6-0s. At the turn of the century virtually all examples of 0-8-0 mineral engines appeared on stone trains, the most numerous being the George Whale G class inside cylinder engines.

Francis Webb retired as Chief Mechanical Engineer of the LNWR in 1903 and was replaced by George Whale. He introduced new designs all of which were used on trains through Penmaenmawr. His first was the 4-4-0 'Precursor'

EX-LNWR push-pull fitted 2-4-2 tank No. 6666 waits to propel its train forward to Llandudno Junction. The old stone built waiting shelter is clearly visible in this 1920s view.

(A.G. Ellis Collection)

class introduced in 1904, a logical development of the old Webb 'Jumbos'. Some of these engines could be seen on trains through Penmaenmawr up to nationalisation. In 1905 came his first 4-6-0 type, the 'Experiment' and a year later the 4-6-0 19' goods mixed traffic engines appeared.

C.J. Bowen-Cooke became C.M.E. in 1909 and he introduced a superheated version of the 'Experiments' known as the 'Prince of Wales' class, as well as another 4-4-0 type in 1910, the 'George the Fifth' class (one of them named *Penmaenmawr*, indeed) and a 4-6-2 tank engine. All of these appeared on the Chester to Holyhead line during the early years of this century, many of them still in service on express and local trains well into the 1930s.

Introduced in 1912, the last express design 4-6-0 for the LNWR, Bowen-Cooke's 'Claughton' class engines 4-6-0s did not appear on Irish boat trains until after World War One because the Civil Engineers at Crewe felt that the track was not of good enough standard to take them. From 1919 onwards 2-8-0s of Great Central design appeared on stone trains from Penmaenmawr sidings after the LNWR had bought thirty of them from the Ministry of Munitions after the end of the Great War. These engines were known as 'M.M.s' or 'Military Marys' by the footplate crews. The Grouping of 1923, when the LNWR became part of the new LMS, had little early effect on motive power through Penmaenmawr - all trains were hauled by locomotives of the old company for the first few years though many changed to red painting. Allocations at Bangor shed which supplied much of the motive power for trains in and out of Penmaenmawr were made up of LNWR engines until the mid-1930s.

The first LMS design to appear through Penmaenmawr was a class of locomotives associated with the Chester and Holyhead line through to the end of steam, the Fowler 4-6-0 'Royal Scots'. These first appeared on 'Irish Mail' trains around 1930, many direct from the manufacturers and without nameplates and were regularly seen in all their guises hauling express passenger trains.

By 1935 locomotives of the LNWR were disappearing rapidly, the only exceptions being 0-8-0 freight engines which worked stone trains periodically through to the mid 1950s and 0-6-0 'Cauliflower' tender engines used on local freight traffic. The last of these went for scrap in 1955. Replacements included 2P inside cylinder 4-4-0s and three-cylinder 'Compound' 4-4-0s of ex-Midland Railway design on semi fast passenger trains. The ubiquitous 'Black 5' 4-6-0s were used on some express workings and sometimes on stone traffic from Penmaenmawr sidings. Other through freight was worked by 4F 0-6-0 tender engines of Fowler design and, for a short while, ex-Lancashire and Yorkshire Railway 0-6-0 tender locomotives. Stone traffic in Penmaenmawr would have included locomotives from other areas on the LMS network, Hughes class 5 2-6-0 'Crabs', Stanier 2-6-0s as well as ex-LNWR 'Super D' 0-8-0s.

Local passenger traffic was handled by 2-6-4 tanks of both Fowler and Stanier design and for a very short time, by ex-Lancashire and Yorkshire Railway 2-4-2 tanks. These engines were not very successful on the North Wales coast and left the area within a few months.

The outbreak of World War Two made no immediate difference to the motive power. There were a few unusual sightings at the station during those years, including a United States Army Transportation Corps 2-8-0 engine on a freight and a streamlined Pacific, No. 6223 *Princess Alice* in dirty condition on a stopping train for Llandudno Junction.

From 1943 the 'Royal Scot' 4-6-0s were withdrawn for rebuilding with taper boilers and, for a while, 'Princess Royal' Pacifics were put on the Irish trains. Holyhead received the

'Royal Scots' immediately after rebuilding and these then monopolised 'Irish Mail' trains, until 1954.

In the years immediately after the war the only new engines to enter service in the area were Fairburn 2-6-4 tanks introduced in 1948 for local passenger trains. Four of these when new were allocated to Bangor shed. Although popular with footplate crews, they were eventually sent to Gourock in exchange for Fowler types which were marginally more powerful and better suited to traffic demands on the North Wales coast line.

Nationalisation in 1948 saw the continued use of ex-LMS engines, including new Ivatt 2-6-2Ts, until British Railways standard designs could be introduced. The first to appear on the North Wales coast were the 'Britannia' Pacifics introduced on 'Irish Mail' trains in 1953. The first five, 70030 to 70034, had BR.1 tenders which were too small for the demands of the service; they were moved quickly to Longsight in Manchester and replaced by 70045 to 70049, with BR.1D tenders of larger capacity.

Other standard designs which appeared on the North Wales coast line in the 1950s included class 5 and 4 4-6-0s, ex War Department 2-8-0s, 4MT 2-6-4 tanks and 3MT 2-6-2 tanks.

The upsurge in holiday traffic during the 1950s saw 'Jubilee' and 'Patriot' 4-6-0s, both in original and rebuilt form on the North Wales coast, staying in the area until the end of steam.

The 1950s also saw the introduction of the 'Land Cruises'. These were worked by Ivatt 2MT 2-6-0s and, until BR class 2s arrived, by ex-Great Western Railway Collett goods 0-6-0s from Pwllheli shed. Another example of this class, No. 3208 was used as a snowplough engine during the winter of 1963; based at Llandudno Junction it often passed through Penmaenmawr station on its way to and from Anglesey. From the late 1950s the solitary 8P Pacific, 71000 *Duke of Gloucester* made a few appearances on the coast line, until withdrawal in 1962.

The introduction of standard designs by BR meant that many older classes were withdrawn; Compounds had all been withdrawn from the North Wales coast by the middle of the 1950s shortly followed by the inside cylinder 2Ps; ex LNWR 0-8-0s and 0-6-0s also disappeared at this time.

The most familiar steam locomotives in the post-War years were the Stanier class 5 4-6-0s; they were used on passenger and freight trains and were often to be found on stone workings from Penmaenmawr. There was an example of the Caprotti type based at Llandudno Junction, sometimes used on various duties around Penmaenmawr. The *Modernization Plan* of 1955 had no immediate effect on motive power in and around Penmaenmawr; there appeared to be no reason to think that things would change in the foreseeable future. The first sign of change came with the arrival of 2 car diesel multiple unit sets (DMUs) on local services. These first appeared on the Llandudno-Blaenau Ffestiniog and Bangor-Amlwch branches in 1956 and on the main line in 1957 when they called at Penmaenmawr on stopping services. These were almost certainly class 101 Metro-Cammell and class 116 Derby units.

Diesel locomotives appeared on test trains through Penmaenmawr in 1958. Electrification on the West Coast main line saw the withdrawal of 'Duchess' Pacifics on Scottish trains by 1960 and many of these engines appeared on the North Wales coast on expresses and even local stopping trains as they neared the end of their working lives. This was the first time that this class of locomotive had appeared in the area in any numbers.

By the early 1960s the BR 9F 2-10-0s were were in use on the stone trains. There is a story that one of these engines came from Llandudno Junction front first instead of tender first, as was usually the case with all locomotives used on stone traffic

Rounding the curve after leaving Penmaenmawr tunnel, 'Princess Coronation' Pacific No. 46256 Sir William A. Stanier FRS hauls an up freight train for Mold Junction on 21st August 1964, something of a comedown after the 'Royal Scot' and other expresses.

(Peter Owen)

BR Britannia Pacific No. 70047 with a local passenger train for Bangor, at the eastern end of Penmaenmawr during the summer of 1964.

(Peter Owen)

The forerunner of the modern container train, headed by an unidentified 'Black Five' heads for Penmaenbach tunnel on its way to Llandudno Junction during 1962.

(Peter Owen)

Introduced on the 'Irish Mail' trains in 1930, the 'Royal Scot' 4-6-0s were associated with the Chester and Holyhead Railway until the end of steam traction. No. 46155 *The Lancer* in rebuilt form approaches Penmaenmawr station with a train for Bangor during the summer of 1964.

(Peter Owen)

Ex-LMS Jubilee 4-6-0 No. 45595 *Southern Rhodesia*, shorn of nameplates, passes Penmaenmawr sea front just east of the station with an evening mail train, shortly before steam traction disappeared from the area in 1965.

(Gwyn Roberts)

BR 9F 2-10-0 No. 92203, the now preserved *Black Prince* owned by the wildlife painter and author David Shepherd, leaves the quarry sidings with a train of railway ballast in the early 1960s.

(Gwyn Roberts)

coming from the east. The shunter pondered the problem of the engine facing the wrong way and decided that the only way to deal with the situation was to detach the tender and place it at the front of the engine. Needless to say this novel solution was not resorted to, though it would have been a very interesting sight.

The influx of diesels was such that by June 1965 all steam locomotives had disappeared from the North Wales coast line, including the sidings at Penmaenmawr. The only steam working after that date, until its return in 1989, was a special excursion to Holyhead for the Altrincham Railway Society, on 21st August 1966. The locomotive used that day was new to the area and this was the only time it was ever seen here, an Eastern Region A2 Pacific No. 60532 *Blue Peter*. Thus it seemed that the curtain had finally came down on 117 years of steam through Penmaenmawr.

Although attempts were made in following years to bring a steam excursion along the North Wales coast line, BR had always resisted, arguing that no turning facilities were available for steam locomotives. Following the success of steam operations on the Cambrian coast line during the summer of 1987, however, BR relented and a three day a week steam service from Crewe to Holyhead has run along the North Wales coast during the summer of 1989. With further excursions to follow in 1990 Penmaenmawr will see steam passing through again after an absence of 23 years. Turning facilities have been arranged at Valley, near Holyhead.

The first steam locomotive to haul a train through Penmaenmawr after all these years was Merchant Navy Pacific *Clan Line*, with a test train on 14th February 1989. It was probably the first Southern Railway engine ever seen in the town. The service operated from June 20th to October 28th and the locomotives used were *Clan Line* and West Country Pacific 34027, *Taw Valley*, another ex-Southern engine, along with Black 5 4-6-0 No. 5407 and LMS Pacific No. 6201 *Princess Elizabeth*. This latter pair in particular brought back fond memories for many locals, and the trips attracted steam enthusiasts from far and wide; a useful vantage point was the 'iron bridge' a structure carrying a footpath a mile east of Penmaenmawr station.

Following the demise of steam traction in 1965 the mainstay of motive power was the class 40 diesel. These were used on the 'Irish Mail' trains, other express passenger services and container traffic for Holyhead. There were also occasional appearances by English Electric type 4 CoCo engines (class 50) particularly as electrification from Crewe to Glasgow developed. Brush type 4 CoCo (class 47) locomotives were a rarity in the area until 1979. After this time, and following the withdrawal of class 40s, they became the principal motive power along the coast. Diesels used on stone trains from Penmaenmawr sidings since the demise of steam have included Sulzer type 2 BoBo (class 24) in the mid 1960s and early 1970s, whilst similar class 25s were frequently used from the mid 1970s, until withdrawal early in 1987. Class 40s were used until their final withdrawal in 1983. Since their disappearance and that of the class 25s, most stone traffic has been put in the hands of class 47s, occasionally helped out by class 31s (Brush type 2 A1A-A1A). With the introduction of regional and railfreight liveries, 47s on stone trains have been seen in Scot-Rail and Inter-City liveries, as well as in Railfreight Grey, standard blue and new blue liveries.

Other diesels seen in Penmaenmawr have included class 33s (BRCWCo), used in 1985 and 1986, class 20s (English Electric Type 1s) around the mid 1970s and, during 1989 in pairs on stone jobs; class 37s, sometimes used on express passenger trains and class 45/1s (BR Type 4 Co Co) introduced on Trans-Pennine trains from 16th May 1983 and seen regularly until the

start of the summer timetable in May 1987. Some of these 'Peak' diesels have been used on stone trains during 1987 but their withdrawal from service on BR network has been rapid and they have disappeared from the area. There has also been the occasional appearance of class 08 0-6-0 diesel shunters, both in the quarry sidings and passing through as light engines to Holyhead and Crewe and Chester. Class 56 (Electroputere and BR type 5 Co Co) locomotives make the occasional visit, usually on test trains and running in turns to Holyhead, sometimes returning light to Crewe.

Local trains were usually made up of 2 car diesel multiple unit sets of all types, particularly class 108 and 101 sets until the introduction of the much maligned 'Pacer' and 150/1 'Sprinter' sets in 1986. From May 1987 class 150/2 'Sprinters' were introduced between Hull and Holyhead. Once the sets came into use, the old DMUs virtually disappeared from local trains serving Penmaenmawr, with the exception of reliefs during the summer of 1987. These trains were usually Tyseley class 116 DMUs and such sets enjoyed something of a revival during 1989.

Motive power in the future may well be in the form of electric traction if pressure applied on BR achieves results. Although BR says that it has no plans to electrify the line from Crewe to Holyhead, the local authorities of Cheshire, Clwyd and Gwynedd have joined forces to look at the feasibility of such a project. BR have already indicated that if these bodies are prepared to finance it then the work could go ahead. Local Members of Parliament, including Ieuan Wynn Jones, the Member for Anglesey, and Sir Anthony Meyer, the Clwyd West MP, have lent support to electrification. Sir Anthony Meyer has argued that the construction of the Channel Tunnel is the perfect opportunity to electrify the North Wales coast line, creating a non-stop service from the Irish ferries at Holyhead through to France. Mr. Wynn Jones has been seeking talks with the Department of Transport and the Welsh Office to see if a joint approach could be made to the EEC for financial support for such a project.

Should finance for electrification be forthcoming then in future years Penmawnmawr could see electric locomotive hauled trains replacing class 47s and electric multiple units replacing the unpopular Sprinter and Pacer diesel sets. Whether electric motive power would be used on stone trains is difficult to predict because the cost of electrifying the sidings may prove expensive and diesel locomotives may be seen as suitable for such traffic.

The first sign that new motive power would be the order of the day was the appearance of diesel multiple units on local services through Penmaenmawr in 1957. These sets were put on local trains until replaced by the new 'Sprinters' and 'Pacers'. Here, two sets make up a train to Manchester leaving Penmaenmawr in the early 1970s.

(Gwyn Roberts)

PROSPECTS

At the 140th Anniversary of the station it is appropriate to consider whether it has much of a future. On the face of it, the prospects look bleak; the loss of station staff is usually the prelude to complete closure if past events in other parts of Great Britain are any guide. Three factors, however, may be influential in keeping the station open. The first is the reopening of Conwy station after 21 years, albeit after Aberconwy Borough Council had financed its rebuilding to relieve road congestion (caused by the construction of the A55 expressway through the town). The same problem of road congestion applies in Penmaenmawr; expressway building continues but the railway is the only means of reaching other places fairly quickly. Thus the station appears to be safe for the present.

The winter of 1984/5 brought with it a further reason for keeping the station open. During January 1985 the frosts and snowfall caused a landside on the mountain to the east of Llanfairfechan, blocking the main A55 road. The only way to pass this obstacle was by rail and this kept the station busy until the blockage was cleared. Should the station close and the same event occur again, there would be no way of by-passing the obstruction.

Perhaps the most important factor is the continued use of the ballast sidings; these are likely to remain open for the foreseeable future for there is enough granite to crush for many years to come.

The three factors put together suggest that the station should remain open, serving the town as it has in the past. There is, however, the attitude of British Rail towards its wayside stations and Government attitudes towards the railway system in general; should British Rail decide that passenger receipts prove insufficient to justify keeping the station open, then they will close it irrespective of its social value and the traffic generated by the quarry sidings. Government policy and its ideas that railways should be self-sufficient by the next century could create an even greater threat to Penmaenmawr station and British Rail could be forced to close it, whether it wished to or not, in order to 'balance its books'.

Assuming that the station remains open, then the next consideration is the building itself. The structure is sound but the upper floor is in fairly poor condition through lack of use. Should demolition occur then it will probably be replaced by a bus shelter structure of the type already existing on the opposite platform. There is, however, a case for putting the building to other uses, as a home or as business accommodation. The buildings adjacent to Llanfair P.G. on Anglesey have been converted successfully by a famous Scottish knitwear manufacturer into a production and sales area, creating employment and increased tourist potential, and there is the possibility that a similar project could be established in the station building at Penmaenmawr. The local Historical Society has asked BR for use of the building as a Museum - they await a reply at time of writing (spring 1990)

The signalbox is at present important; it controls stone traffic entering and leaving the sidings but in future years with increasing computerisation there is the possibility that all traffic could be controlled from Llandudno Junction. The box at Penmaenmawr, along with that at Aber, could be closed. A member of the station staff suggested in 1989 that this may happen within the next three years.

The story of the railway station at Penmaenmawr has reflected the fortunes of the town, and its quarries. While its future may be uncertain, its past influence has been very important to the town which it has served.

From small beginnings the station and its surroundings grew to meet the demands required of it and as those demands lessened, then facilities were reduced accordingly. Perhaps the most important asset for the station has been the quarrying industry and the production of railway ballast, so essential for providing a sound base on which to lay the track and for the smooth running of trains. The good quality of the Penmaenmawr stone was recognised in the last century and this is still the case today.

If you travel through Penmaenmawr by train perhaps on the way to the ferry to Ireland from Holyhead, as you pass through the station with its complex of sidings and the mountain with its quarries, I hope that this book will have helped you consider the past importance of the town both as tourist and quarrying centre and the humble ballast which makes your journey so smooth and comfortable. Perhaps you will consider alighting at this little station, the centre of so many developments over the years, and to visit Penmaenmawr-see for yourself the all-important quarries above, which have contributed so much to the life and times of both town and railway.

Replacements for ageing dmus appeared during 1986 in the form of class 142 'Pacers' and class 150/1 'Sprinters'. Here 'Pacer' No. 142048 leaves Penmaenmawr for Llandudno Junction on a cold March day in 1987.

(Gwyn Roberts)